Berklee Practice Method

VIOLA

Get Your Band Together

MATT GLASER
MIMI RABSON

and the
Berklee Faculty

Berklee Press

Editor in Chief: Jonathan Feist
Vice President of Online Learning and Continuing Education: Debbie Cavalier
Assistant Vice President of Berklee Media: Robert F. Green
Dean of Continuing Education: Carin Nuernberg
Editorial Assistants: Dominick DiMaria, Sarah Walk

ISBN 978-0-87639-131-0

DISTRIBUTED BY

1140 Boylston Street
Boston, MA 02215-3693 USA
(617) 747-2146

Visit Berklee Press Online at
www.berkleepress.com

HAL•LEONARD®
CORPORATION
7777 W. BLUEMOUND RD. P.O. BOX 13819
MILWAUKEE, WISCONSIN 53213

Visit Hal Leonard Online at
www.halleonard.com

DESIGN TEAM

Matt Marvuglio	Curriculum Editor
	Dean of the Professional Performance Division
Jonathan Feist	Series Editor
Rich Appleman	Chair Emeritus of the Bass Department
Larry Baione	Chair of the Guitar Department
Jeff Galindo	Assistant Professor of Brass
Matt Glaser	Artistic Director for the Center for American Roots Music
Russell Hoffmann	Associate Professor of Piano
Charles Lewis	Associate Professor of Brass
Jim Odgren	Professor of Woodwinds
Tiger Okoshi	Professor of Brass
Bill Pierce	Chair of the Woodwind Department
Tom Plsek	Chair of the Brass Department
Mimi Rabson	Associate Professor of Strings
John Repucci	Assistant Chair of the Bass Department
Ed Saindon	Professor of Percussion
Ron Savage	Chair of the Ensemble Department
Casey Scheuerell	Professor of Percussion
Paul Schmeling	Chair Emeritus of the Piano Department

The Band

Rich Appleman	Bass
Larry Baione	Guitar
Jim Odgren	Saxophone
Mimi Rabson	Viola
Casey Scheuerell	Drums
Paul Schmeling	Keyboard

Music composed by Matt Marvuglio

Recording produced and engineered by Rob Jaczko, Chair of the Music Production and
    Engineering Department

Contents

CD Tracks

Basics

CD 1. Tuning Note A

Chapter I. Playing Rock ("Sweet")

CD 2. "Sweet" Full Band

CD 3. "Sweet" First Part

CD 4. "Sweet" Second Part

CD 5. "Sweet" Call/Response 1

CD 6. "Sweet" Call/Response 2

CD 7. "Sweet" You're the Viola

Chapter II. Playing Blues ("Do It Now")

CD 8. "Do It Now" Full Band

CD 9. "Do It Now" Slides

CD 10. "Do It Now" You're the Viola

CD 11. "Do It Now" Call/Response 1

CD 12. "Do It Now" Call/Response 2

CD 13. "Do It Now" Call/Response 3

Chapter III. Playing Blues Swing ("I Just Wanna Be With You")

CD 14. "I Just Wanna Be With You" Full Band

CD 15. "I Just Wanna Be With You" You're the Viola

CD 16. "I Just Wanna Be With You" Call/Response 1

CD 17. "I Just Wanna Be With You" Call/Response 2

Chapter IV. Playing Funk ("Leave Me Alone")

CD 18. "Leave Me Alone" Full Band

CD 19. "Leave Me Alone" You're the Viola

CD 20. "Leave Me Alone" Funk Hookup 1

CD 21. "Leave Me Alone" Funk Hookup 2

CD 22. "Leave Me Alone" Call/Response 1

CD 23. "Leave Me Alone" Call/Response 2

CD 24. "Leave Me Alone" Intonation

Foreword

Berklee College of Music has been training musicians for over fifty years. Our graduates go onto successful careers in the music business, and many have found their way to the very top of the industry, producing hit records, receiving the highest awards, and sharing their music with millions of people.

An important reason why Berklee is so successful is that our curriculum stresses the practical application of musical principles. Our students spend a lot of time playing together in bands. When you play with other musicians, you learn things that are impossible to learn in any other way. Teachers are invaluable, practicing by yourself is critical, but performing in a band is the most valuable experience of all. That's what is so special about this series: it gives you the theory you need, but also prepares you to play in a band.

The goal of the *Berklee Practice Method* is to present some of Berklee's teaching strategies in book and audio form. The chairs of each of our instrumental departments—guitar, bass, keyboard, percussion, woodwind, brass, and string—have gotten together and discussed the best ways to teach you how to play in a band. They teamed with some of our best faculty and produced a set of books with play-along audio tracks that uniquely prepares its readers to play with other musicians.

Students who want to study at Berklee come from a variety of backgrounds. Some have great technique, but have never improvised. Some have incredible ears, but need more work on their reading skills. Some have a very creative, intuitive sense of music, but their technical skills aren't strong enough, yet, to articulate their ideas.

The *Berklee Practice Method* teaches many of these different aspects of musicianship. It is the material that our faculty wishes all Berklee freshmen could master before arriving on our doorstep.

When you work through this book, don't just read it. You've got to play through every example, along with the recording. Better yet, play them with your own band.

Playing music with other people is how you will learn the most. This series will help you master the skills you need to become a creative, expressive, and supportive musician that anyone would want to have in their band.

Gary Burton
Executive Vice President,
Berklee College of Music

Preface

Thank you for choosing the *Berklee Practice Method* for viola. This book/CD package, developed by the faculty of Berklee College of Music, is part of the *Berklee Practice Method* series—the instrumental method that teaches how to play in a band.

The recording included with this method provides an instant band you can play along with, featuring great players from Berklee's performance faculty. Each tune has exercises and practice tracks that will help prepare you to play it. Rock, blues, and funk are just some of the styles you will perform.

The lessons in this book will guide you through technique that is specific to playing a viola in a contemporary ensemble. When you play in a band, your primary concern is with melody, improvising, playing the groove, and understanding chords. This is very different than traditional classical playing, and it will be a major part of this method. This book is intended for viola players who know how to read notes and basic rhythms, and play all major scales and some arpeggios. Ideally, this method should be learned under the guidance of a private teacher, but viola players learning on their own will also find it invaluable.

Most important, you will learn the skills you need to play viola in a band. Play along with the recording, and play with your friends. This series coordinates methods for many different instruments, and all are based on the same tunes, in the same keys. If you know a drummer, guitarist, horn player, etc., have them pick up the *Berklee Practice Method* for their own instruments, and then you can jam together.

Work hard, make music, have fun!

Matt Glaser, Artistic Director for the Center for American Roots Music
Mimi Rabson, Associate Professor of Strings
Berklee College of Music

Basics

Before you begin, you should understand the following topics.

PLUGGING IN

In a band, instruments are generally amplified. A device, such as a microphone or pickup, carries the sound to either an amplifier or a mixer.

In the past, a violist's options for amplification were limited, but in recent years, the technology has come a long way, and you have a number of good choices: microphones, pickups, or electric violas.

To protect your equipment and your ear drums, follow these steps when you use an amp or mixing board. It is similar for all kinds of electrification.

1. Turn off the amp and set the volume down to 0.

2. Plug your cable into your mic, pickup, or viola and then into the amp.

3. Turn on the amp.

4. If you are using a pickup or electric instrument, turn up your instrument's volume all the way.

5. Play at a medium volume. Slowly, turn up the amp or mixer volume until it is loud enough.

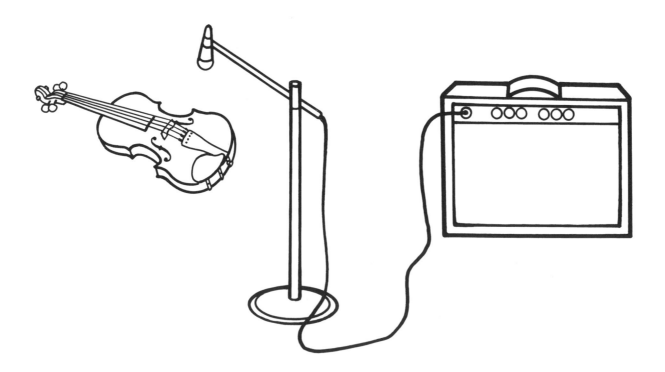

Microphones

Most varieties of microphones work well for violas; a regular dynamic microphone will work fine. You can also use a "lavelier" mic that clips onto your viola. Better quality microphones will give you a better sound.

Some microphones need batteries, and some require "phantom power" from a mixer or preamplifier. Be sure you understand how your mic is powered, before you buy it.

What you need: A mic, an XLR cable, an XLR-to-1/4" converter, a mic stand (if it's not a stick-on mic), and an amplifier (or a sound system). Some mics require batteries or a "phantom power" source; check with your dealer regarding how your mic is powered.

Cost: $50 to $5000

Pros: It's easy, and you don't have to modify your acoustic viola.

Cons: There is a great danger of feedback, especially if you are playing with a loud band. Never point your mic at your amplifier or the sound system's speakers.

If you use a microphone, position it a few feet away from your instrument to get a warmer sound. Close miking will give you a rawer sound, which you may want for certain types of music.

Pickups

A pickup, or "transducer," transforms your strings' vibrations into an electronic signal. This signal can then be directed to an amplifier. Some pickups slip into the opening on the side of your bridge, some stick to the bridge, and some stick to the body of the instrument.

Some pickups are built into the bridge or the soundpost. These should be installed by a repair technician.

What you need: A pickup, a 1/4" cable (also called a "guitar cord"), and an amplifier. Some pickups come with their own cable.

Cost: $100 to $500 (plus installation, if needed)

Pros: It's easy, and there is less chance for feedback.

Cons: Your instrument may no longer sound like a viola. It may sound more like some kind of space sax with a cold. This can be corrected with reverb and other effects (see "amplifiers and effects" in the following sections).

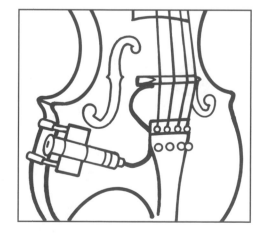

Electric Violas

Guitar players have used electric instruments for decades. Electric violas are similar. They have their pickups built in, so you can just plug them in and play. A *hollow body* electric viola can be used as an acoustic viola, if necessary. These instruments are prone to feedback. *Solid body* instruments require amplification, but they eliminate all possibility of feedback.

What you need: An electric viola, a 1/4" guitar cable, and an amplifier.

Cost: $350 to $3000

Pros: No feedback. Since the shape of the instrument is no longer necessary for sound production, there are some really cool-looking instruments out there that come in lots of colors. Also you can get 5- and 6-string instruments as well. Unplugged, these instruments are good for quiet practicing.

Cons: Again, the sound will not bring Stradivarius to mind.

If you use an electric viola or a pickup, you will probably have a wire coming out of your instrument. Keep it out of the way by running it over your shoulder.

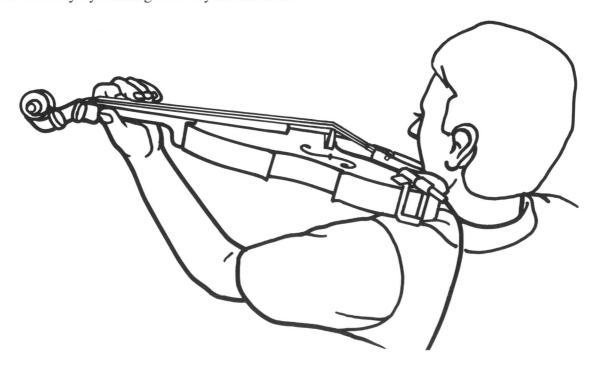

Other Gear

Once your sound is in an electric signal, various other pieces of gear will help you modify its volume level or timbre.

- **Amplifiers**

Amplifiers boost the volume of the electronic signal coming from your mic, pickup, or electric instrument. An amp will make the electronic signal loud enough to play in most situations. There are lots of amplifiers on the market, and since all electronic instruments use them, it's easy to find them used.

Once you have electrified your sound, take your viola to your local music store and have them show you around the amps. You'll notice most amps have some kind of tone controls: bass, treble, mid range, or maybe a more complex kind of equalization (EQ). These controls accentuate different frequencies of your sound. Try them out to get the sound you like the best. Often, the treble control needs to be turned down, to get a good viola sound.

You can get a little amp that clips onto your belt for $35. The price goes up from there. A good amp that produces a fairly realistic viola sound will cost from $250 to $600 new. Amps can be heavy, so you may want to get some kind of luggage rack to carry it around.

- **Volume pedals**

A volume pedal is a useful, though optional, piece of equipment. With a touch of your foot, it will allow you to get loud enough to play a solo, and then afterwards, come back down to ensemble volume. Or to suddenly go into a loud section after a quiet beginning. They cost $30 to $80 and are well worth it.

- **Effects**

Once you can actually be heard in your band, you may want to start altering your sound with distortion, reverb (short for "reverberation"), compression, pitch shifting, flanging, wah-wah, and so on. Violists can use the same effects devices as those used by guitar players.

The list of things you can do is huge. There are "stomp boxes" that range in price from $50 to $200. Stomp boxes generally have one kind of effect, which you can control with a foot pedal. Other devices do what several stomp boxes would do, all in one machine. These are a little more expensive.

Some machines can be programmed to do what you tell them. There are pedal boards for the floor, devices that clip to your belt, and lately, some that you can plug into your computer that use effects stored on the Internet. Again, since guitarists use the same ones, most music stores have a number of effects devices for you to try.

Final Thoughts on Gear

The world of electronics is vast and fairly untapped by violists. Ask fellow electric musicians what they are using. Get friendly with your local music store and keep up with what's new. There are several good magazines and catalogs that can keep you up to date with the latest sounds. If you don't like the sound you are getting, you can easily change it with a new EQ setting, a different amp, a new stomp box, or a new pickup. Explore!

This technology is always changing. Whatever you buy today, there will be a better one in six months that will probably cost less than what you paid for yours. Luckily, there is a large used market in the world of music electronics. The prices quoted here are for new gear, but there are lots of great buys to be had in the used market. And if you do buy new, you can usually sell your old gear and get some of your money back.

When you play using amplification, you will need to carry more gear around with you. Keep a couple of extra guitar cords and 9-volt batteries (for stomp boxes) in your case. You never know when one will stop working or someone else will need to borrow one.

Finally, remember your ears. Amplification lets you play loud, but you have to be careful. You only have one pair of ears, and if they get broken or damaged, you can't fix them. If you really have to play loud, use earplugs. Permanent hearing loss is a common problem among rock musicians.

Learning More

Though you won't generally find a variety of pickups and violas at your local music store, they are gradually becoming more common. Check out various string-oriented magazines and Web sites for sources of dealers. School music teachers may have information about different publications or where to buy instruments and accessories.

PERFORMANCE HEALTH

Athletes rely on several kinds of specialists whose job it is to make sure that they are in peak physical condition. Coaches and trainers help them warm up before practice and cool down afterwards. If they get injured, they get benched until they are better.

Although playing music isn't football, it is a strenuous physical activity. Many talented people fall by the wayside because they don't take care of their bodies.

You have to be your own coach and make sure you are relaxed and warmed up before you play, and that you cool down sufficiently after you play. If you're in any pain, bench yourself. If the pain persists more than a couple of days, seek professional help. Too many people are out of the game before it starts because they didn't take care of themselves. Don't let that happen to you.

The best thing you can do to preserve your performance health is to maintain a healthy posture and hand position. This is one of the reasons why having a teacher is so important. A teacher, like an athlete's coach, will make sure that you are moving in a healthy way.

Whether you are sitting or standing, the posture of your upper body should be in the same position. Your back should be straight but relaxed. Keep your shoulders down, and play with as little tension as possible. You should feel comfortable and at ease at all times while playing, whether sitting or standing. Keep the viola parallel to the floor, and shift its weight between your left hand and shoulder. Do not grip or tense up. Relax.

Sitting

Standing

TUNING

Before you play, tune your strings to the right notes. If your string is flat (too loose), tighten its tuning peg to raise the pitch. If your string is sharp (too tight), loosen its tuning peg to lower the pitch. As you get close to the right pitch, listen for *beats* (tiny waves of sound) as you play your note along with the correctly tuned note. Slight differences in pitch causes these audible beats. Keep tuning until you don't hear any beats.

There are many ways to tune. One of the most convenient is using an electric tuner. You can also tune by ear, using this recording.

Tuning to the *Berklee Practice Method* Recording

1. Listen to track 1, "Tuning Note A."

2. Play your A string. Determine whether the pitch of your A string is above or below the recorded pitch. Don't worry if you can't tell, at first. Just turn the A string's peg slowly, in either direction, until it sounds right.

3. While your string is still sounding its note, turn the A string's tuning peg until it is at the same pitch as the tuning note on the recording. Pluck it again every few seconds to keep it sounding its current pitch, until it is tuned.

4. When this string is tuned, tune the C, G, and D strings.

Your viola should now be in tune.

NOTATION

Notes are written on a staff.

Viola music is usually written using the "alto clef" staff. Here are the notes for the lines and spaces in alto clef.

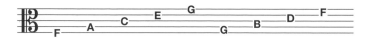

Ledger Lines

The staff can be extended with ledger lines.

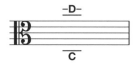

ACCIDENTALS

Accidentals are symbols appearing before notes, showing that a pitch is raised or lowered for the duration of the measure, unless otherwise indicated.

♭	Flat	Next note down (half step)
♯	Sharp	Next note up (half step)
♮	Natural	Cancels a flat or sharp

SCALES: MAJOR AND MINOR

Scales are patterns of notes, presented sequentially in a single octave. Two common types of scales are the major and minor scales.

C Major

C Minor

KEY SIGNATURES

Key signatures indicate a tune's key and show which notes always get sharps or flats. Accidentals on the lines and spaces in the key signature affect those notes unless there is a natural sign. Here are some key signatures used in this book.

| C Major | F Major | G Major | D Major |
| A Minor | D Minor | E Minor | B Minor |

RHYTHMS

Here are some basic rhythms. When there are no actual pitches, as in a clapping exercise, rhythms may be shown on the *percussion clef*. (The beats are numbered below the staff.)

Connect notes using a tie. The first note is held for a total of six beats.

Extend a note's rhythmic value by using a dot. A dot increases the value by one half.

Triplets squeeze three even attacks into the space of two. In this example, the quarter-note beat is divided first into two eighth notes, and then into three eighth-note triplets.

RHYTHMIC NOTATION

Music that just shows rhythms may be written in rhythmic notation. This is common for rhythm exercises when you clap or tap your foot, without sounding any specific pitches.

Whole note   Half notes   Quarter notes   Eighth notes   Sixteenth notes

MEASURES

Groups of beats are divided into measures. Measure lengths are shown with *time signatures.*
This measure is in ♩4/4 time; there are four quarter notes in the measure.

In 12/8 time, there are twelve eighth notes per measure.

ARTICULATIONS

Articulations give more information about how to play a note. Here are four common ones used in this book:

>	Accent	Loud
.	Staccato	Short
^	Short accent	Short and loud
–	Long	Hold for full value

SHIFTING

Shifting is the technique that string players use to move their hands up and down the fingerboard. Several of the exercises in this book require the ability to shift as denoted by the fingerings that are written above the notes. If you haven't learned to shift yet, we suggest you find a teacher to work with you to ensure that you develop the best possible techinque.

Now, let's play!

"Sweet" is a *rock* tune. Rock started in the 1960s and has roots in blues, swing, r&b, and rock 'n' roll. There are many different styles of rock. To hear more rock, listen to artists such as Rage Against the Machine, Melissa Etheridge, Korn, Paula Cole, Bjork, Tori Amos, Primus, Jimi Hendrix, Led Zeppelin, and violinists Jean-Luc Ponty, Boyd Tinsley (Dave Matthews), Jerry Goodman (Mahavishnu Orchestra), Papa John Creach, and Don "Sugar Cane" Harris.

LESSON 1
TECHNIQUE/THEORY

Listen to "Sweet" on the recording. The viola and saxophone play the melody together. Use of the "distortion" effect gives the viola sound a hard-rock edge. This tune has two parts.

In the first part of the melody, the violist plays these notes. Use your ear to find the rhythms.

In the second part, the viola plays these notes.

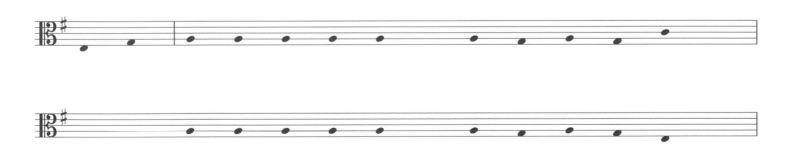

Play along with the recording, and try to match the melody. Notice that there is a short introduction before the first part begins.

1

Melodies such as "Sweet" are created out of different *licks*—short, melodic figures or *phrases*. A musical phrase is similar to a phrase in spoken or written language. It is a continuous musical idea that is unbroken and uninterrupted by long rests or periods of silence. Phrases can be short licks, or they can be extended melodies.

In "Sweet," the viola and lead guitar play the melody, and the other instruments play other kinds of parts. The parts all sound good together because the melody, the *chords* (three or more notes sounded together), and the *groove* (rhythmic time feel) all work together.

ARTICULATION

Articulation is the way a note is played—short, long, accented, and so on. Choosing good articulations for your notes and phrases will make your melodies come alive.

On a viola, different articulations are played by changing the way you use your bow. Changing the way you *attack* (start) and *release* (stop) the sound changes the note's articulation.

Legato

Notes in the first part of "Sweet" flow together smoothly. This is *legato* style articulation, often notated with a *slur* marking (⌣) . Each note is held for its *full rhythmic value* so that it leads right up to the next note. Though violists use slurs to indicate bowings, other instruments use them to indicate phrasing, so try to determine who added the slurs to the notation and why. They may or may not make sense as bowings.

When you play legato notes, try to minimize the space between the notes. You can do this by playing all the notes in one bow or by making smooth bow changes between the notes.

Practice legato long tones with the recording. Only change bows every two measures, where you see a comma ('). Count in your head while you play, and make sure you hold each note for its full value. Then try a smooth bow change on each note.

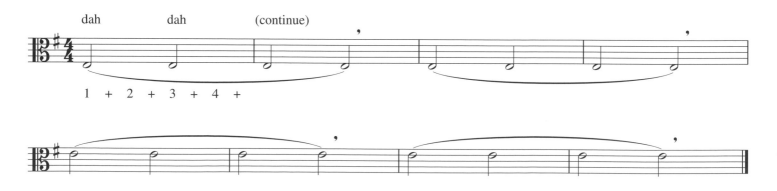

Practice the first part of "Sweet" using legato articulation, using the same track. The notes within each phrase should sound connected. What bowings would you use to make them legato?

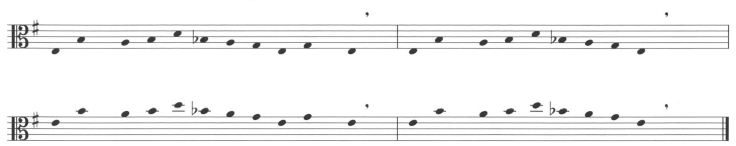

Staccato

Notes in the second part to "Sweet" are much shorter and more separated. The opposite of legato (long) is *staccato* (short). Staccato notes are indicated with a dot (˙). To play staccato, use separate bows for each note. Use the middle or lower half of the bow for a stronger sound. Make a little accent at the beginning of each note by pressing with the index finger of your bow hand. Make a clean release at the end of each note in the same way.

Staccato notes are not held for their full rhythmic value, and there should be space between notes. Staccato quarter notes are written like this:

These notes sound much shorter than quarter notes—more like sixteenths. Here is the same line written as sixteenth notes. As you can see, the dots are much easier to read than the sixteenth-note flags with dotted-eighth-note rests.

Practice staccato articulations with the recording, one note per beat. Though the notes are short, you should still think about phrasing, and take your bow off the string between phrases rather than between notes.

LISTEN **4** PLAY

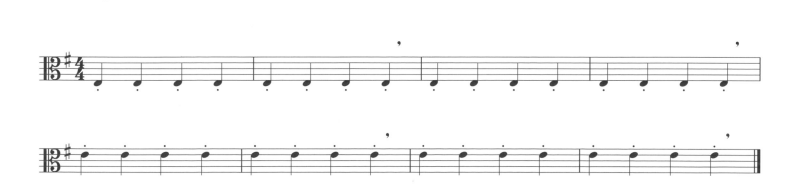

Now practice staccato eighth notes with the recording. Try this in two different ways.

1. The first time you play this exercise, keep your bow on the string the whole time.

2. The second time, "brush" the string with the bow, lifting it on either side of the note.

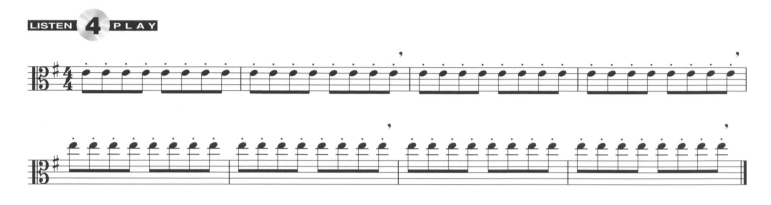

The licks in the second part of "Sweet" each have three notes that are played staccato on the recording. The other notes shouldn't be as short. Practice these licks a few times to get the staccato feel, and then practice it with the recording.

PRACTICE TIP

Keep your bow on the string, except during rests. If you play a combination of short and long notes, this makes it much easier to play accurate rhythms and stay in the groove.

LEAD SHEETS

Articulations may be marked in formal, published music. When you play in a band, more often, you will use informal music that only shows chord symbols and melody, usually with no articulations, no phrasing, and no other expressive markings. This is called a *lead sheet*. Finding the right articulations will be up to you.

This is what the first part to "Sweet" looks like on a lead sheet.

The whole band may read the same lead sheet. Each player will use it differently to create a part for their instrument. As a viola player, one way you will use the lead sheet is to read and play the song's melody.

The keyboard, guitar, and bass all play parts using notes from the chords. By tuning in to the chords, you'll find it easier to keep your place in the music. When it's your turn to *solo* (improvise), the chord symbols will be useful to you as well, as we will see in later chapters.

Different bands will create different parts for the same tune. This is one of the coolest things about lead-sheet notation: it leaves room for individual interpretation.

You will see the full lead sheet to "Sweet" in lesson 4.

LESSON 2
LEARNING THE GROOVE

WHAT IS A GROOVE?

A *groove* is a combination of musical patterns in which everyone in the band feels and plays to a common pulse. This creates a sense of unity and momentum. The *rhythm section* (usually drums, bass, guitar, and keyboard) lays down the groove's dynamic and rhythmic feel. A violist or other soloist also contributes to the groove and performs the melody based on this feel.

Listen to "Sweet." As is common in hard rock, the groove to "Sweet" has a strong, clear pulse, and a loud, forceful sound. The drums play a heavy, repetitive beat. The bass outlines the harmonic structure. The rhythm guitar and keyboard play chords. The viola and lead guitar play the melody. Everyone uses the same rhythms, though often at different times. This makes the whole band sound like one unit; they're all *hooked up* with the groove.

In lesson 1, when you played along with the recording and matched the viola part, you hooked up with a groove and became part of the band.

Viola in a Groove

On our recording of "Sweet," the violist has two roles in the groove: melody and improvisation. If there were several violas, or other strings, there might be a third kind of role: that of a member of a string section. In a section, the strings may play chords together, or they may all play the same melody in *unison* (at the same time). In a smaller band, like the one on our recording, there is only one viola player. This player is *out front*, and at the center of attention.

Rock music has included strings for a long time. Bands such as the Beatles used them back in the 1960s. In those days, strings were generally used more in the backgrounds of rock bands, rather than up front. With technology such as electric instruments and better pickups, strings are becoming more common in the rock scene.

HOOKING UP TO ROCK

As a violist, though you are not a member of the rhythm section, you are still part of the groove and must tap into its rhythmic feel. The way you play should help the other band members feel the beat or pulse you feel.

The way to hook up to a groove is by learning its unique pulse and rhythmic feel. Then, your playing will hook up rhythmically with the rest of the band. Your phrasing and articulation will help you define the rhythms of the melody and hook up to the groove.

The best thing to do is to latch on to one of the parts in the rhythm section: bass, keyboard, or even just the snare drum. Imitate its sound and feel as you play.

PRACTICE TIP

Use clear bow strokes. Think about the beginnings and the endings of each note you play. Play each note like a snare drum hit.

LISTEN 3 PLAY

Count along with the beat, repeating "1, 2, 3, 4" through every measure. While you count, play a very short note along with the snare drum on the *backbeat*—beats 2 and 4, where you see the circles below. A strong backbeat is one of the characteristics of rock grooves.

PRACTICE TIP

To create a good percussive sound while working on these rhythm exercises, try dropping your bow on the string near the frog. The "chops" require a little practice. They work best on the lower strings. Try not to sound a particular pitch; it should be more like a snare drum hit. The more you control the drop, the better your rhythm will be.

LISTEN 3 PLAY

While you "chop" and count, tap your foot on the quarter-note pulse.

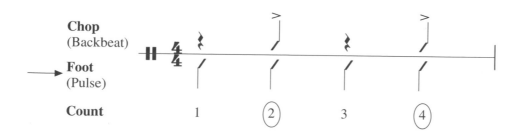

This tune has a sixteenth-note feel, so change your counting to sixteenth notes, matching the cymbals. On each beat, count evenly, "1 e + a, 2 e + a, 3 e + a, 4 e + a" (say "and" for "+"). Try saying this first at a slower tempo, without the recording, until you get the hang of it. When you are ready, play the recording and say the syllables in tempo.

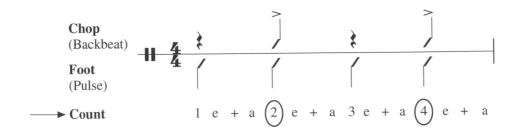

Play the rhythm of the viola's first part to "Sweet" using only the note E. Tap your foot on the quarter note, and feel the sixteenth-note *subdivisions* (divisions within a beat). When you are ready, do this along with the recording. The same phrase is played twice. Try singing the melody along with the CD at the same time.

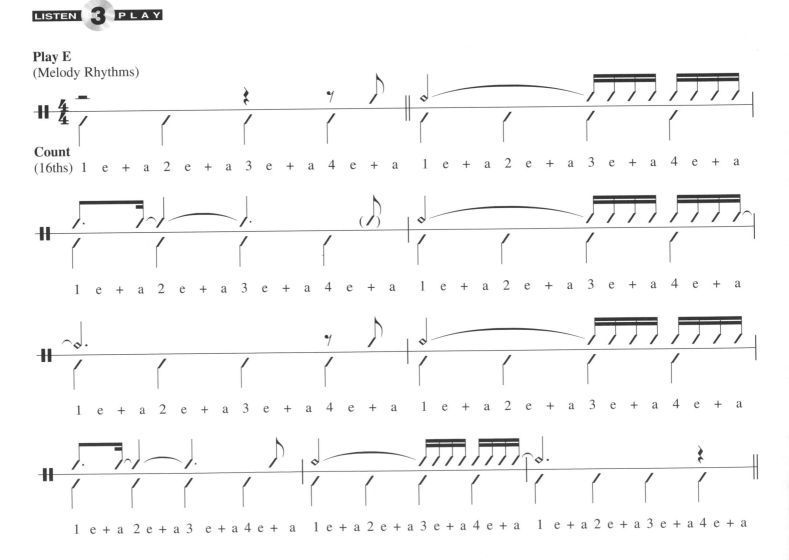

Play the actual part along with the recording. Tap your foot, and feel the sixteenth notes as you play. Use legato articulations, and hook up with the groove.

Listen to the second part to "Sweet," find the pulse, and count along. When you are ready, play an A along with the recording. The same rhythmic lick repeats, played a total of eight times.

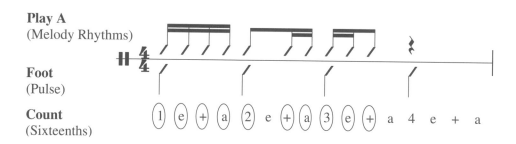

Play the actual part along with the recording. Tap your foot and count in your head as you play. Watch your articulations, and hook up with the groove.

Finally, play both parts of the melody, following your ear and not looking at the music. Make sure to use different articulations on each part, and hook up with the rhythm section. When the viola solos, sit back and listen, and continue to feel the groove. Come in again when the melody returns.

LESSON 3
IMPROVISATION

Improvisation is the invention of a solo. When you improvise, you tell the story of what you think about the tune, and what it means to you. Though an improvised solo may seem spontaneous to the audience, the musician probably did a lot of preparation before performing it. There are three things you must know before you start improvising: the song melody, when you should solo, and what notes will sound good in your solo.

FORM AND ARRANGEMENT

When you are preparing to improvise on a tune, start by learning how it is organized. This will let you know when you should start your improvised solo and where the chords change.

LISTEN **2** PLAY

Listen to "Sweet" and follow the viola. After an introduction by the rhythm section, the viola plays the melody. Then, there is an improvised viola solo. Finally, the viola plays the melody again, followed by a short ending.

During the improvised solo, you can still feel the written melody. That's because the improvisation follows the same chords as the written melody. This repeating chord structure is the same throughout the entire tune, and is called the song's *form*—its plan or structure.

A common way to show this organization is with a *chord chart*. Chord charts don't show rhythm or pitch, just measures and chord symbols. The slash marks (/ / / /) mean "play in time."

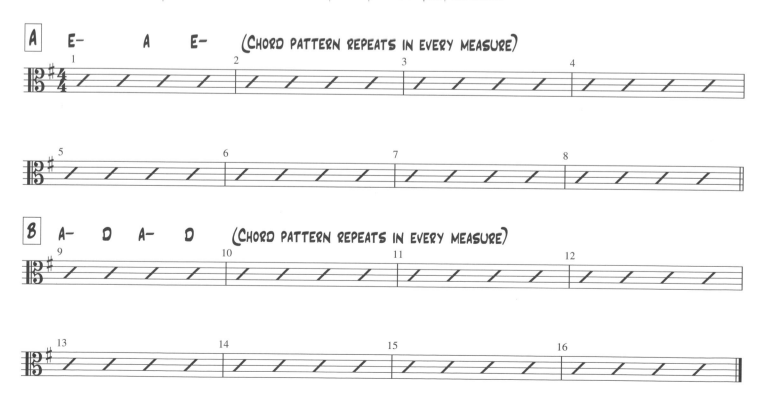

The chord chart makes it easy to see that the form of "Sweet" is sixteen measures long. It has two primary musical ideas: the first eight measures present the first idea (Idea "A"), with the **E– A E–** patterns. The second eight measures present the second idea (Idea "B"), with the **A– O A– O** patterns. This form can be described simply as "AB" or "AB form." These letters help us remember the form, freeing us from having to read while we're performing.

HEAD/CHORUS

One complete repetition of this form is called a *chorus*. A chorus can feature the written melody, in which case it is called the *head*, or it can feature just the chord structure, supporting an improvisation. The word *chorus* is also used to mean a song section that is alternated with varying verses. In this book, however, the word "chorus" is only used to mean "once through the form."

ARRANGING "SWEET"

Your band can choose how many choruses you want to play, and create your own *arrangement* of "Sweet." The number of choruses depends on how many players will improvise when you perform the tune. On the recorded performance of "Sweet," only one player solos (the viola), playing for two choruses. Often, several members of the band will take turns playing choruses of improvised solos. A solo can be one or two choruses, or even more.

On the recording, the same basic arrangement is used for all the tunes: the head, an improvised viola solo, and then the head again. There are often short introductions and endings as well.

Listen to "Sweet" and follow the arrangement. This is the arrangement for "Sweet" played on the recording:

INTRO	HEAD	VIOLA SOLO: 2X	HEAD	ENDING
4 MEASURES	1 CHORUS = 16 MEASURES	1 CHORUS = 16 MEASURES	1 CHORUS = 16 MEASURES	2 MEASURES

When you play "Sweet" with your band, you can play your own arrangement, adding extra solo choruses, different endings, or other changes.

IDEAS FOR IMPROVISING

When you improvise, some notes will sound better than others. There are many ways to find notes that will sound good. You can use the notes from the tune's melody, you can use notes from the chords, and you can use notes from scales that match the tune. Eventually, this becomes intuitive, and you can just follow your ear.

Scales: E Minor Pentatonic

The violist on this recording of "Sweet" built much of her solo using notes from a *pentatonic scale*. Pentatonic scales are among the simplest and most versatile types of scales in all of music. All pentatonic scales have five notes. There are two common types of pentatonic scales: major and minor. For "Sweet," the soloist used the *minor pentatonic scale* built on E. This scale works well here because the tune is in the key of E minor. Notice that the E is repeated, up an octave, to close the scale.

Use this scale to create your improvised licks. You only need a few notes to create a lick, so divide the scale into halves. Use one half for some licks and the other half for other licks. This will add contrast between them.

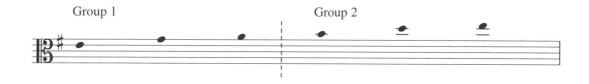

Here are some of the licks that can be created using some notes from these groups.

You may have noticed that all of these licks use the same rhythm. This is the rhythm used above.

Plugging different notes into the same rhythm is another good technique for building solos. It makes the licks sound related, like part of the same thing. You don't need to use the same exact rhythm every time, but some repetition can be very effective.

CALL AND RESPONSE

Listen to each phrase, and then play it back, echoing it exactly. Each lick comes from the E minor pentatonic scale, using the groupings and the rhythm discussed above. Slashes ("/") in measures marked "play" mean that you should play in time during those measures. Listen carefully, and hook up with the groove.

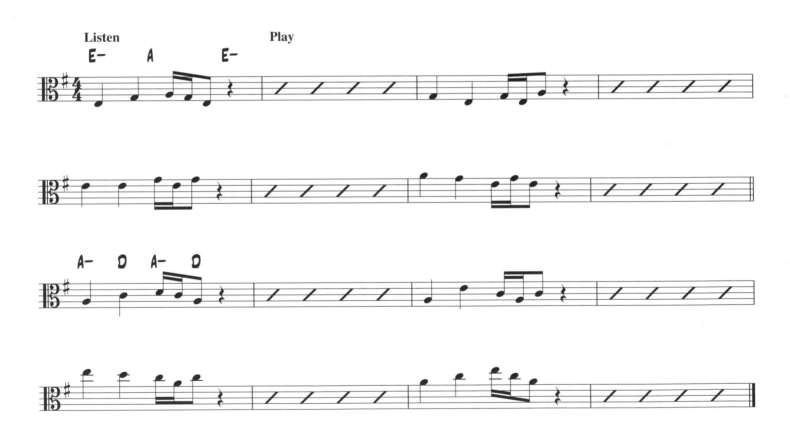

Keep practicing that track until you can echo all phrases perfectly. Then do the same thing for the phrases on this next track.

Play the same two tracks again. This time, instead of echoing the phrases exactly, answer them with your own improvised phrases. Use the same rhythms, and only use notes of the E minor pentatonic scale.

Write out some of your own licks, like the ones you have been playing. Don't worry about perfecting your notation; just sketch out your ideas. This will help you remember them when you are improvising.

> ### PRACTICE TIP
>
> A good solo combines two elements: rhythmic drive and melodic content. Combine that with your unique musical personality, and you've got it.

LISTEN **7** PLAY

Create a 1-chorus solo using any techniques you have learned. Memorize your solo, and practice it along with the recording.

PLAY IN A BAND TIP

When playing in a band, listen to the other players' parts, and try to create a musical conversation. This makes playing much more fun, and more musical too. When you are improvising a solo, listen to what the other instruments are playing. They will suggest many ideas that you can use in your solo, such as rhythms and licks, and you will inspire each other. When someone else is soloing, try to find a place in the rhythm section by imitating the rhythm players and using those percussive "chops."

LESSON 4
READING

When you play in a band, sometimes you will get a viola part that shows exactly what you should play. Other times, you may get a lead sheet, giving you more freedom to create your own part. You should be able to play from either one.

VIOLA PART

Below is a written viola part to "Sweet." This part shows articulation markings and rehearsal letters.

HARD ROCK   Style indication. This tune is hard rock, and you should play it in that style: heavy bass, strong beat, sixteenth-note feel, and other elements typical of that hard-edged sound.

♩ = 86   Metronome marking. This tells you how fast you should play this tune. If you have a metronome, set it to 86, and play "Sweet" at that tempo.

INTRO   Introduction. The written part begins with an introduction, which is made up of four measures of the B section.

3   A bar with a number over it means that you should rest for that number of measures. The introduction begins with just the rhythm section, so you can sit out. But count along, so you are ready to come in on the pickup to letter A.

[A]   Rehearsal letter. These are different than form letters, which you saw in lesson 3. These letters help you when you are practicing with other musicians because everyone's parts have the same letters marked at the same places.

‖: :‖   Repeat signs. Play the music between these signs twice (or more).

[A9]   Rehearsal letter with measure number. These mark different areas within a chorus. Again, this can be helpful during rehearsals.

AFTER SOLOS, REPEAT TO ENDING
When the soloists are finished, play the head one more time, and then proceed to the measures marked "Ending."

ENDING   A final section that is added to the form. End the tune with these measures.

Play "Sweet" along with the recording. Follow the viola part exactly as it is written.

LISTEN **7** PLAY

SWEET

Viola

By Matt Marvuglio

After solos, repeat to ending

Ending

TIP

Sometimes, slurs are phrasing marks, not bowings. Change bowings as needed, especially when you are the only one playing the part. Use bowings to match the sound of the phrasing.

LEAD SHEET

Lead sheets present the chords and melody, and they are usually written in treble clef. Lead sheets give you more interpretive freedom than full formal viola parts do. Notice that there is no written introduction on this lead sheet. The introduction you hear in the recording is an interpretation of the lead sheet by that band. Your band should create your own unique arrangement.

SWEET

By Matt Marvuglio

"Hard Rock" ♩ = 86

PLAY IN A BAND TIP

As you rehearse "Sweet," follow the lead sheet. It will help you keep your place in the form.

CHAPTER I
DAILY PRACTICE ROUTINE

ARTICULATION PRACTICE

Legato

Practice these two legato exercises along with the recording to the first part of "Sweet." Change your bow only where you see the breath marks. The notes should sound almost connected to each other.

> **PRACTICE TIP**
>
> Keep your bow on the string all the time. Try to make the changes of bow smooth by keeping your bow hand very flexible.

LISTEN 3 PLAY

Legato Exercise 1

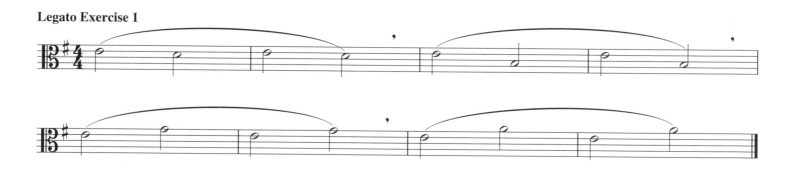

Legato Exercise 2

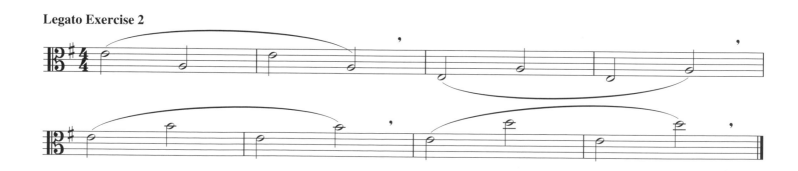

Staccato

Practice the E minor pentatonic scale along with the recording, using staccato articulations. Listen to the drums, and try to play your notes exactly in time.

Staccato Exercise 1

Staccato Exercise 2

SCALE PRACTICE

Here are the notes of the E minor pentatonic scale through two octaves. When you are comfortable playing all of these notes, you'll be able to use them when you improvise.

In lesson 3, you divided the scale into two groups of three notes. There are other ways to group notes of this scale. For example, you can take groups of four consecutive scale notes, beginning on any scale degree. This next exercise shows you many different ways of grouping notes, and helps you master the E minor pentatonic scale throughout the viola's register. Practice it with both legato and staccato phrasing. This exercise is based on the form of "Sweet," so you can practice it along with the full track, playing it several times. Begin after the introduction.

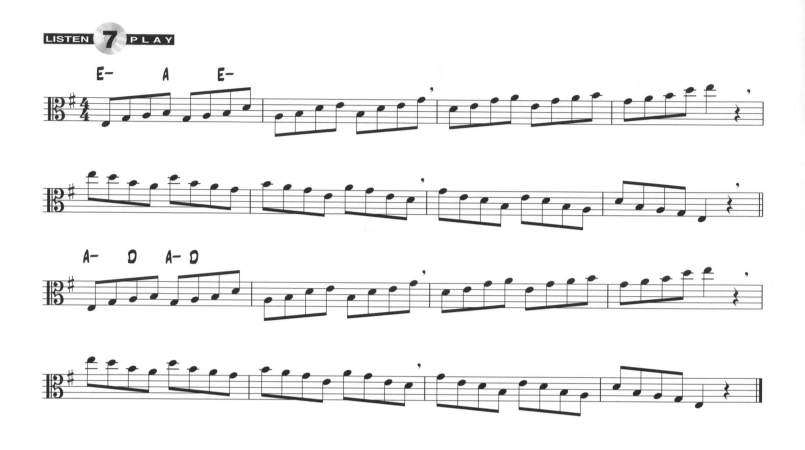

IMPROVISATION PRACTICE

This exercise will help you practice improvising. You will use groups of notes from the E minor pentatonic scale and a rhythmic pattern, just like you did in lesson 3. The difference is that now you will be creating improvised licks while the music is playing.

Before you play, you must do two things. First, you must choose your groups of notes. For now, we'll use the same groups from lesson 3.

Group 1   Group 2

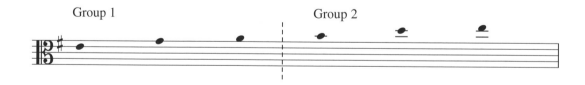

Second, you must choose a rhythmic figure. Again, we'll start with the one from lesson 3.

Here's how it works. You will be improvising with the rhythm section. In odd measures, you will play; in even measures, you will plan. When you plan, decide what you will play, choosing what notes to use in the rhythm above, choosing notes alternately from groups 1 and 2. Before you begin, plan your first measure. It will be organized like this:

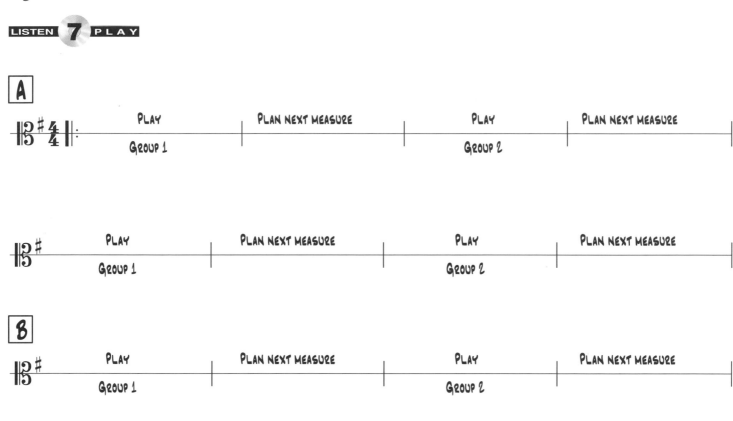

When you are comfortable with that, use different groups of notes and different rhythms. For groups of notes, choose some from the pentatonic exercise earlier in this section. For rhythms, you can use any of these, or write your own. Just keep it simple, and be strict in following it.

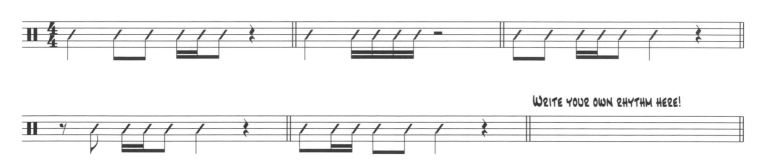

CHALLENGE

Choose different rhythms or note groups for the A section and for the B section. When you play along with the track, play the melody at the first and last chorus, as it is played on the recording.

SOLO PRACTICE

Practice this solo along with the recording. Notice that much of it is based on the E minor pentatonic scale.

MEMORIZE

Memorizing the licks and melodies from these exercises will help you play the tune, especially when you improvise. What you practice helps you when you perform. But performing is the best practice, so get together with some other musicians and learn these tunes with your own band.

Memorize the viola part to "Sweet." Also memorize the lead sheet. The "Summary" shows everything you need to play "Sweet" from a lead sheet. Memorizing it will help you memorize the tune.

> ### PRACTICE TIP
> Write out your own exercises based on the E minor pentatonic scale. The more ways you find to make melodies from that scale, the more you make music that's truly your own!

SUMMARY

FORM
16-BAR AB
(1 CHORUS = 16 BARS)
A: 8 M.
B: 8 M.

ARRANGEMENT
INTRO: 4 M.
1 CHORUS MELODY
2 CHORUS SOLO
1 CHORUS MELODY
END: 2 M.

HARMONY
A   E- A   B   A- D

SCALE
E MINOR PENTATONIC

PLAY "SWEET" WITH YOUR OWN BAND!

"Do It Now" is a *blues* tune. Blues began in the late 1800s, and it has had a profound influence on American music styles, including rock, jazz, and soul. To hear more blues, listen to artists such as B.B. King, the Blues Brothers, Robben Ford, Bonnie Raitt, James Cotton, Albert King, and Paul Butterfield.

LESSON 5
TECHNIQUE/THEORY

Listen to the recording of "Do It Now" and play along. Try to match the viola. The melody has three lines. Each starts differently but ends the same.

First Line

Second Line

Third Line

PRACTICE TIP

In melodies, look for patterns—notes that are the same or similar from one phrase to the next. In "Do It Now," the three phrases end exactly the same. Also, the first two phrases are very similar, with the only difference being that the first A-natural in the first phrase changes to an A-flat in the second. As you learn songs, notice what remains the same and what's different. You'll learn them faster.

SLIDES

Articulations, such as slides, can help you get a good blues sound in your playing.

If you listen to great blues singers, you may notice that they slide into some notes and slide off of other notes. Sometimes, they slide around a bunch of notes while singing just one syllable. This is called "melismatic singing." To get this sound on the viola, practice sliding into some notes and off of others.

Play along with the following track, and try to imitate the exact sound and length of the slides.

LISTEN **9** PLAY

LESSON 6
LEARNING THE GROOVE

HOOKING UP TO A BLUES SHUFFLE

LISTEN **8** PLAY

Listen to "Do It Now." This groove has its roots in traditional r&b, gospel, and jazz. The feel is often called a *12/8 shuffle* because of the twelve eighth notes in each bar. (The drums play these on the ride cymbal or hi-hat.)

Tap your foot on every beat, and count triplets: "1 trip-let 2 trip-let 3 trip-let 4 trip-let." The basic pulse (tap) is on the quarter note. However, each pulse also has an underlying triplet that divides the beat into three equal parts. "Chop" the triplets on your viola.

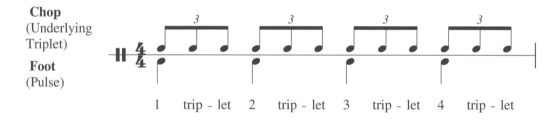

This triplet feel is part of what makes the beat a *shuffle*. While all shuffles don't include triplets on every single beat, the underlying triplet *feel* is always present.

The triplet is a fundamental aspect of all swing and shuffle beats. Understanding and feeling the concept of "subdivisions" (dividing the pulse into smaller rhythms) will help you play many other kinds of grooves.

"Do It Now" begins with the drums playing two beats of triplets. This establishes the shuffle groove. Listen for the steady triplet beat in the hi-hat, and find the triplet patterns in the other instruments. Listen to the bass part. Which beats have a triplet feel? Is the triplet pattern the same in every measure or does it change?

SWING EIGHTH NOTES

Eighth notes in shuffle grooves are usually played as triplets, even though they are notated as *straight* eighth notes.

Though these rhythms look different, in some musical styles, they are played the same. The notated part to "Do It Now" shows eighth notes notated like this:

Since it is a shuffle tune, they are played more like this:

The part is easier to read without the triplet markings on every beat, and the rhythms are played as triplets even though they are notated as if they were regular eighth notes. Interpreting rhythms in this way is called "swinging the eighth notes." Swing eighth notes are common in many styles of music, including blues, jazz, and swing.

Sometimes, the word "swing," "swing feel," or "shuffle" appears on the lead sheet, telling you how to play eighth notes. If there is no such indication, try it both ways and choose which fits the groove best. The style of the tune may help you choose whether to swing your eighth notes or play them straight.

Listen again to "Do It Now," and play the viola part along with the recording. Feel the triplets on every beat, listen to the drums, and hook up with the groove.

LESSON 7
IMPROVISATION

Listen to "Do It Now," and follow the form. The form of this tune is called a *12-bar blues*.

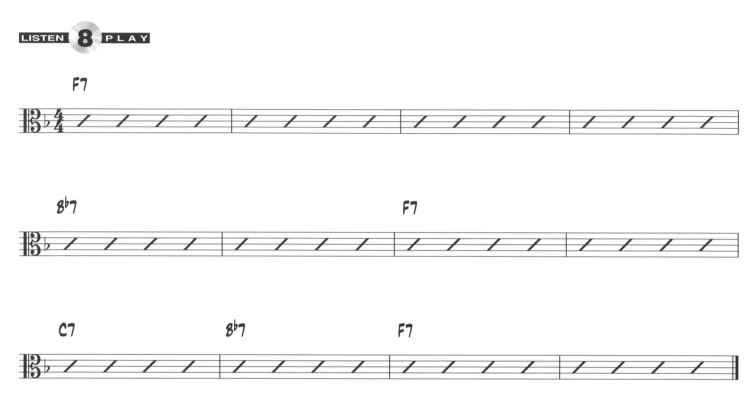

A 12-bar blues has three 4-bar phrases. It is common for the first two phrases in the melody to be similar and the third one to be different. This form is very common in many styles of music, including jazz, rock, and funk.

In "Do It Now," the first phrase has four bars of the I chord (F7). The second phrase has two bars of the IV chord (B♭7) followed by two bars of the I chord (F7). The third section has one bar of V (C7), one bar of IV (B♭7), and then two bars of I (F7). This is typically the way that chords move in blues.

Memorize the blues form and chord progression. You will see it again many times throughout your career.

About the Blues

The blues is the great aquifer that underlies all American music. Jazz, rock 'n' roll, country, and r&b are all continually fed by this giant river called the blues. If you're going to play any kind of popular music, you'll have to get used to playing the blues.

The blues is many things. In general, it's the expression of a sad feeling or playing music to make that sad feeling better. It's also a musical form, as discussed above. In vocal versions of the blues, the first two lyric lines are usually the same, and the third is different.

> *I'm gonna' buy myself a brand new pair of shoes.*
> *I'm gonna' buy myself a brand new pair of shoes.*
> *I'm gonna' quit singing those doggone hard-time blues.*

Here's a way to generalize about this form:

> *The second phrase of the blues is the same as the first.*
> *The second phrase of the blues is the same as the first.*
> *The third phrase of the blues is almost the same as the first.*

ARRANGEMENT

"Do It Now" begins with the drum playing two beats of triplets. This is called a *pickup*—a short introduction, less than a measure long, that leads to a strong downbeat. Here is the arrangement played on the recording.

PICKUP	HEAD: 2x	VIOLA SOLO: 2x	HEAD	ENDING
| 2 Beats Drums	|: 1 Chorus = 12 Measures :||	: 1 Chorus = 12 Measures :|	1 Chorus = 12 Measures ||	4 Measures ||

> **PRACTICE TIP**
>
> When you listen to any music, figure out the arrangement. How long is the head? Is there an introduction or an ending? How many solo choruses does the band take?

SCALES: F BLUES SCALE

In chapter 1, you created licks using the E minor pentatonic scale. Here is the F minor pentatonic scale:

The *F blues scale* has just one more note—the flat fifth degree (B-natural):

Practice the notes of the F blues scale over the range of your viola. Extend it, if you can. This scale is difficult on the viola because it has three notes that are right next to each other (chromatic neighbors). If you are sliding the same finger between two notes, make sure to change your bow stroke at that moment; otherwise, you'll get a sliding sound that you may not always want. This slide can be a nice blues effect, though, so practice it both ways.

CALL AND RESPONSE

In these call-and-response exercises, divide the F blues scale into two groups. The B-natural will be used in both groups. The first chorus draws from group 1, and the second chorus draws from group 2. The notes of each group can be played in any octave.

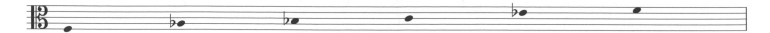

Use this rhythm for each lick.

1. Echo each lick exactly as you hear it.
2. Improvise an answer to each lick. Use the same rhythm for each answer, but choose your own notes.

Use notes from group 1 in this chorus.

LISTEN **11** PLAY

Listen   Play

LISTEN **12** PLAY

Use notes from group 2 in this chorus.

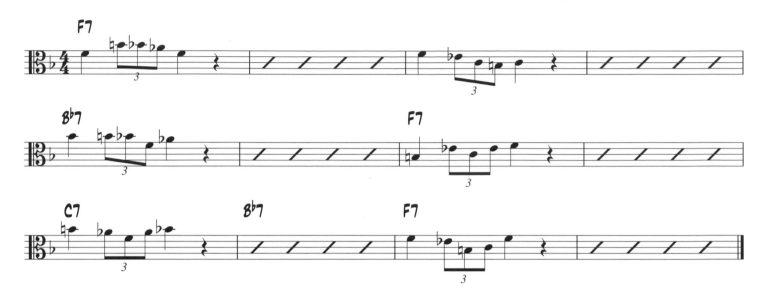

LISTEN **13** PLAY

Use notes from groups 1 or 2 in this chorus, choosing the same group as you hear on the recording.

Write out a few of your own ideas. Use notes from the F blues scale.

LISTEN **10** PLAY

Create a 2-chorus solo using any techniques you have learned. Memorize your solo, and practice it along with the recording.

LESSON 8
READING

VIOLA PART

This *chart* (written part) uses symbols and instructions that direct you to skip around the pages. When you get the hang of these symbols, you will see that they help reduce the number of written measures, and make the chart easier to read quickly, at a glance. Sometimes, these directions are called the chart's *road map*.

2 BEATS DRUMS Pickup. Short introduction (less than a measure).

𝄋   Sign. Later, there will be a direction (D.S., or "from the sign") telling you to jump to this symbol from another location in the music.

⊕   Coda symbol. "Coda" is another word for "ending." On the last chorus, skip from the first coda symbol to the second coda symbol (at the end of the piece). This symbol may also have the words "To Coda," or other directions (such as "last time only"). Often, you will just see the coda symbol by itself.

D.S. AL CODA From the sign (𝄋), and take the coda. Jump back to the sign (first measure, after the pickup), and play from there. When you reach the first coda symbol, skip ahead to the next coda symbol (at the end).

AFTER SOLOS When all solo choruses are finished, follow this direction.

B   Different choruses may be marked with different letters. In this tune, the head is marked "A," and the improvisation choruses are marked "B."

SOLO   Solo chorus. Play this part when other musicians in the band improvise. When you play this tune with your own band, you might repeat this section several times, depending on how many people solo. When you solo, then obviously, you won't play this written part.

Play "Do It Now" along with the recording, and follow the written viola part exactly. Even if you have it memorized already, follow the part as you play.

Do It Now

Viola Part

By Matt Marvuglio

LEAD SHEET

Now play "Do It Now" with the recording, and work from the lead sheet.

Do It Now

By Matt Marvuglio

"Medium Shuffle" ♩ = 96

BLUES SCALE PRACTICE

Viola Register: High Notes/Low Notes

Playing in different registers will give you new tone qualities and sounds. A phrase played in the low register has a certain energy and intensity. The same phrase played an octave higher will have a different feel and sound.

Practice this register exercise, and when you are ready, practice it along with the recording. Notice the different characters between the registers.

VIOLA PLAYERS AND CHORDS

Guitar and keyboard players often play *chords*—three or more notes sounded simultaneously. The viola can play chords, but more often, it will play the notes one after another, or as *arpeggios*.

"Do It Now" uses three different *dominant seventh* chords in its chord progression. Play them on your viola.

Chord tones (the notes of a chord) are important resources for notes when you improvise, similar to scales. Practice playing the chord tones for the chords in "Do It Now," using rhythms that fit the song's feel. Remember to swing your eighth notes. When you are ready, play this exercise along with the recording.

LISTEN 10 PLAY

SEVENTH CHORD EXERCISE 2

These exercises will help you develop your skills playing dominant seventh chords. It is in *descending form*— moving from high to low. Swing your eighth notes. Practice each chorus until you can play it easily, and then practice it with the recording.

LISTEN 10 PLAY

The second exercise presents dominant seventh chords in *ascending form*—moving from low to high.

SOLO PRACTICE

Practice the first chorus of the solo to "Do It Now" along with the recording, reading the noteheads below. Use your ear to find the right rhythms.

When you can play this solo, play the full tune without looking at the music—first the melody, then the solo (play the above chorus twice), and then the melody again to end it. Follow your ear, and try to match the viola on the recording.

PERFORMANCE TIP

If you make a mistake or get lost, keep your composure, and pretend that everything is going fine. Listen to the other instruments, hear what chords they are playing, and find your way back into the form. You can even practice getting lost and then finding your place. Start the recording at a random point within the track, and then follow your ear.

MEMORIZE

Create your own solo using any techniques you have learned. Memorize your part, and then play through the tune with the recording as if you were performing it live. Keep your place in the form, and don't stop, whatever happens.

LISTEN **10** PLAY

SUMMARY

FORM	ARRANGEMENT	HARMONY	SCALE
12-BAR BLUES	PICKUP: 2 BEATS DRUMS	F7 B♭7 C7	F BLUES
(1 CHORUS = 12 BARS)	2 CHORUS MELODY		
	2 CHORUS SOLO		
	1 CHORUS MELODY		
	END: 4 M.		

PLAY "DO IT NOW" WITH YOUR OWN BAND!

"I Just Wanna Be With You" is a *blues swing*. *Swing* is a dance-oriented, big-band style from the 1930s. To hear more swing, listen to artists such as Count Basie, Benny Goodman, the Squirrel Nut Zippers, Diana Krall, Branford Marsalis, Kevin Eubanks, Joanne Brackeen, Cherry Poppin' Daddies, and Big Bad Voodoo Daddy.

LESSON 9
TECHNIQUE/THEORY

Listen to "I Just Wanna Be With You," and then play it along with the recording. This tune is a minor blues, similar to "Do It Now." The viola is doubled by the guitar. Look for similarities between the three lines.

LISTEN 14 PLAY

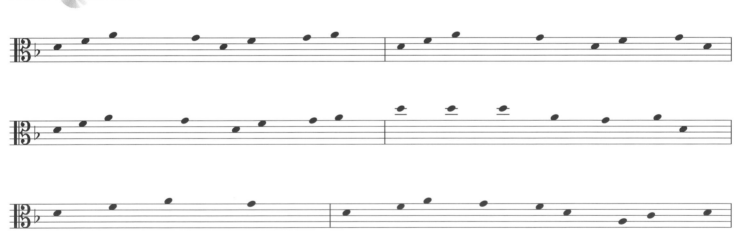

PICKUPS

Each phrase of "I Just Wanna Be With You" begins on a weak beat (an eighth note before beat 4), leading to a strong beat (beat 1). Notes leading to a strong beat are called *pickups*. While you are preparing to play, count beats along with the rhythm section. This will help you come in at the right time.

Feel the pulse and count out loud. You come in after the third beat.

ARTICULATION: ACCENTS

Notes marked with accent (>) articulations are played louder than the rest so that they stand out. They are often the highest notes in the phrase.

Accents can make a phrase sound more spirited and energize a performance. Use them sparingly. If every note is accented, then nothing will stand out.

Practice accents along with the recording. Make accented notes stand out from the unaccented notes.

LISTEN **15** P L A Y

Accenting some of the notes in "I Just Wanna Be With You" will make the melody come alive—especially accenting notes that are unexpected, on beats that would ordinarily be weak, such as any eighth note off a beat, or beat 4. Practice it along with the recording. Make your accented notes stand out from the others.

LISTEN **15** P L A Y

PRACTICE TIP

Practice slowly. Before you can play something fast, you must be able to play it slowly.
Practice your fingerings, and try to hear the notes in your head before you play them.

LESSON 10
LEARNING THE GROOVE

Listen to "I Just Wanna Be With You" and focus on the cymbals. This tune is a shuffle, like "Do It Now." There is a triplet feel under each beat. The main difference is that in this tune, the middle note in the triplet is left out. This is common in swing.

LISTEN **14** PLAY

| Shuffle
("Do It Now") | Swing Shuffle
("I Just Wanna...") |

This syncopated "push-pull" feel is basic to jazz and r&b. Sometimes this feel is called a "double shuffle" because the drummer plays the same rhythm with both hands. In swing, the bass player usually plays a "walking" quarter-note bass line.

> ### PRACTICE TIP
>
> Record your practice. Use a laptop or digital recorder, and record yourself playing along with the CD. Then listen to your recording. How accurately and consistently are you playing?

HOOKING UP TO SWING

Listen to "I Just Wanna Be With You." Find the beat, tap your foot, and chop along with the backbeat.

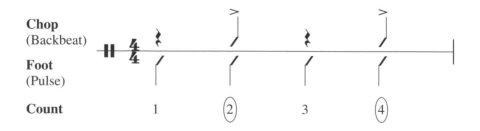

This tune has a swing feel, so count triplets on each beat as you play along with the backbeat. When you are ready, do this along with the recording. The circles show where to bow. The hi-hat matches your counting.

LISTEN 14 PLAY

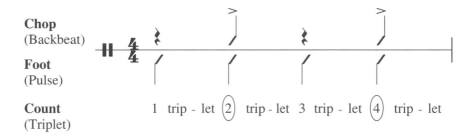

Play swing eighth notes (see lesson 6).

LISTEN 14 PLAY

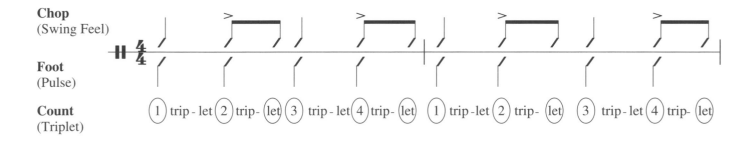

LEARNING "I JUST WANNA BE WITH YOU"

In this tune, the final note of the first measure is accented. Notes on the ordinarily weak beat 4 are usually not stressed, so this comes as a surprise—an interruption of the expected pulse. A rhythm such as this is called a *syncopation*. Syncopation is an important part of swing.

Bow the actual rhythms of the melody on your open D-string. When you are ready, bow along with the recording. Accent the notes that are marked.

Chop
(Melody
Rhythms)

Foot
(Pulse)

Count
(Triplet)

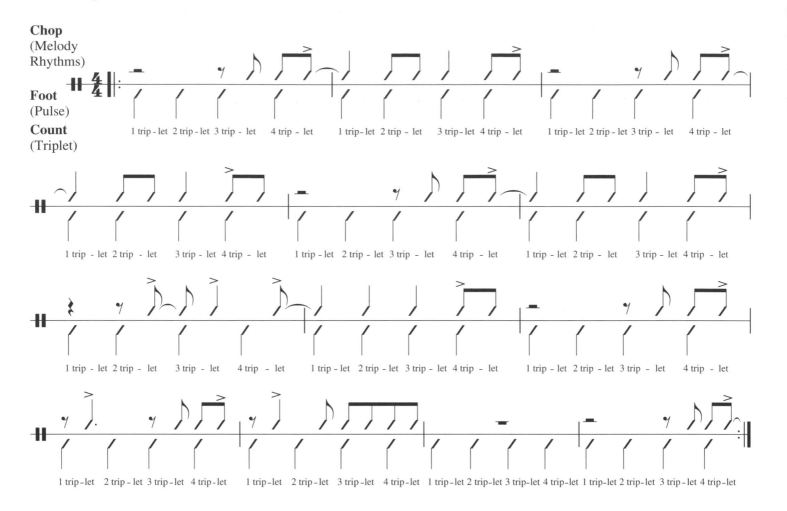

Play the actual part along with the recording. Tap your foot and count in your head, as you play. Use accents, and hook up with the groove.

LESSON 11
IMPROVISATION

FORM AND ARRANGEMENT

Listen to "I Just Wanna Be With You" and follow the form. This tune is another 12-bar blues. The form of each chorus is twelve measures long and divided into three phrases, just like "Do It Now." Is there an introduction or ending? What part of the form did these added sections come from?

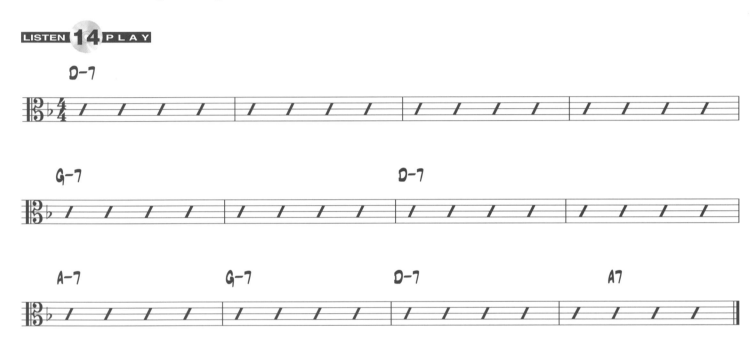

This is the arrangement used on the recording:

The intro and ending come from the form's last four measures. On the recording, the band chose to play the ending twice. This kind of repeated ending is called a *tag ending*.

PERFORMANCE TIP

Sometimes, a band may decide to "tag a tune" (play a tag ending) several times, building energy with each repetition. If things are going well and everyone is in the mood, a band may even make an ending longer than the rest of the tune. This is a place where people really let loose and have fun playing. When you listen to music, pay attention to what a band is doing at the end of a tune.

IDEAS FOR IMPROVISING

Scales: D Blues Scale

The D blues scale is a good one for this tune. Play it on your viola.

Practice the notes of the D blues scale over a wider range. Notice that it starts on an A. If you can, extend this range even higher.

D Blues Practice

LISTEN **15** PLAY

Practice the D blues scale through this big melodic range, up and down, with the recording. Play each note in steady time, one per beat, and play as evenly as you can. Some notes, especially blue notes such as the A-flat, will jump out at you. Use these notes when you create your own solo.

When you're playing the melody, watch out for the rhythm in bar 6. Three notes in a row start on the "and" of the beats, not on the beats themselves. This syncopation is a very important rhythmic part of swing.

CALL AND RESPONSE

1. Echo each phrase, exactly as you hear it.

2. Improvise an answer to each phrase. Imitate the sound and rhythmic feel of the phrase you hear, and use the notes from the D blues scale.

LISTEN **16** PLAY

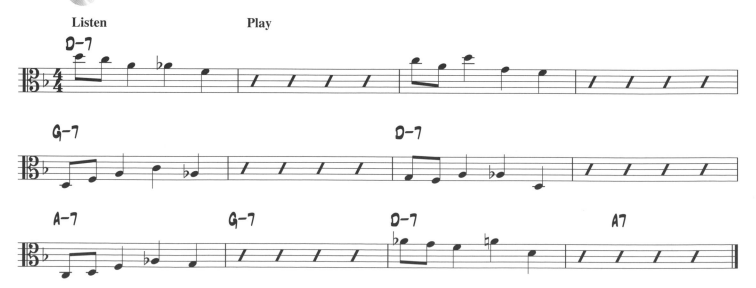

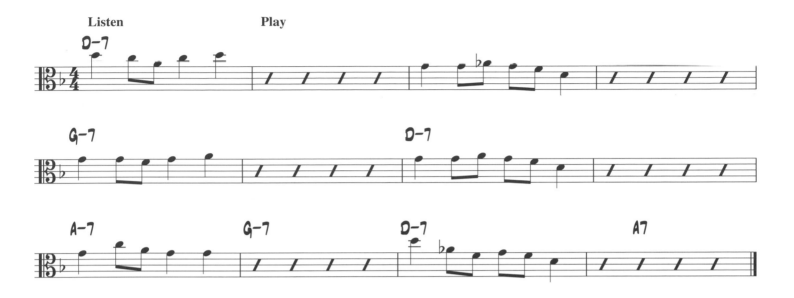

Write out a few of your own ideas. Use the D blues scale.

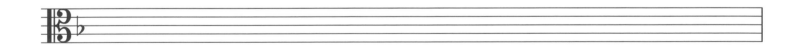

Create a 2-chorus solo using any techniques you have learned. Memorize your solo, and practice it along with the recording.

VIOLA PART

Play "I Just Wanna Be With You" while reading from the written viola part. Play it as written. The guitar doubles the viola at the melody and plays chords during the improvisation choruses.

I Just Wanna Be With You
Viola Part

By Matt Marvuglio

LEAD SHEET

Play "I Just Wanna Be With You" from the lead sheet.

INTRO/ENDING Though this lead sheet doesn't show an introduction or ending, you and your band can create your own. The intro can be just drums, as you saw in "Do It Now," or it can come from the last line of the tune, as it does on the recording of this tune. Tag the ending at least three times, repeating the last four measures of the written part.

Since the melody is relatively short in length (twelve measures), you might want to play it twice when you are playing this tune with your own band. Play the pickups whenever you play the melody. You may or may not want to include them in your solo. If you are the only one in your band playing melody, try it up an octave.

LISTEN 15 PLAY

I JUST WANNA BE WITH YOU

By Matt Marvuglio

CHAPTER III
DAILY PRACTICE ROUTINE

ARTICULATIONS: CONSONANTS AND STACCATO (SWING STYLE)

LISTEN **15** PLAY

Memorize the written melody, copying the phrasing and articulation of the violist on the recording. How short or long are the notes? How do the notes begin? Imitate the sound and feel of the recorded melody as precisely as you can, and find ways to make your bow re-create the exact sound of each note.

When you are learning by ear, think about how each note begins. Notice that the notes on this tune often start with a hard sound, like P, T, or K. We call these note beginnings *consonant* sounds because they're the opposite of vowels, which are soft and fluid. Consonant sounds are harder and distinct. For consonant sounds, grab your string with the bow, and begin the note with a little "pop." This helps to define your notes rhythmically. Try to create this popping sound using different parts of your bow.

This sound is very common in swing, particularly on short, staccato notes. In swing, staccato is marked with a (^). To play this articulation, your bow should grab the string with a "popping" sound.

Practice swing staccato articulation along with the recording. In this exercise, the staccato markings help emphasize the backbeat. Be sure to start each note with a consonant articulation.

LISTEN **15** PLAY

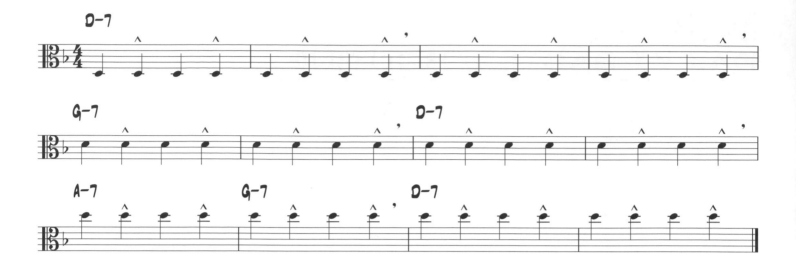

When you play viola in a band, you use the instrument in a very rhythmic way. So be creative with your bowing, and make the music as rhythmic and alive as possible.

The recorded version of "I Just Wanna Be With You" uses a combination of staccato and accented notes. Articulating these notes differently energizes the whole melody line. Try to make each articulation stand out. Practice the articulations as shown, and then play it along with the recording.

LISTEN 15 PLAY

VIOLA SOUND

Imagining different "syllables," such as "tah," "tut," and "hut," will help you imagine different ways your bow can make a sound.

Practice long tones on your viola every day, and try to get as full and as warm a sound as you can. Here is an example of the kind of exercise you should do regularly. This one combines practicing long tones with practicing the D blues scale. Keep repeating this exercise for the whole track.

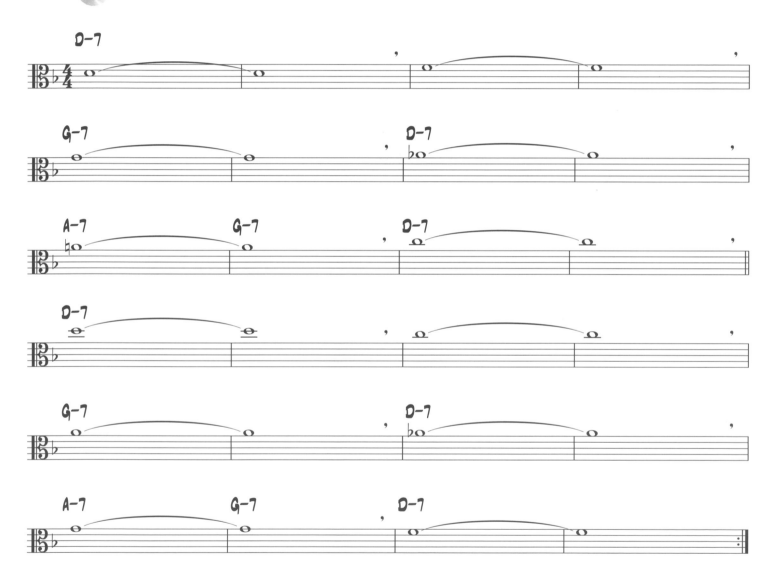

IMPROVISATION

Chords

The lead sheet to "I Just Wanna Be With You" includes four different chords. The first three are *minor seventh chords* and the last one (**A7**) is a *dominant seventh* chord. The improvised solo makes good use of chord tones.

Practice chord tones with the recording. Notice how different the dominant seventh chord (**A7** in the last measure) sounds—especially its note C-sharp. The different chord sound and the change in the groove make the last measure stand out and give the tune a unique character. It also helps the last measure to lead back to the first measure for when the form repeats. This is called a *turnaround* because it "turns the form around" back to the beginning.

LISTEN **15** PLAY

Improvising Using Chord Tones

LISTEN 15 PLAY

Practice this viola solo, and then play it along with the recording. Notice the use of chord tones.

Create some of your own chord-tone licks.

LISTEN 15 PLAY

Create a 2-chorus solo using any techniques you have learned. Memorize your solo, and practice it along with the recording.

SOLO PRACTICE

LISTEN 15 PLAY

Practice the recorded viola solo to "I Just Wanna Be With You." When you are ready, play along with the recording.

MEMORIZE

Work on playing your own, personal interpretation of the melody of "I Just Wanna Be With You," with your own articulations and phrasing. Record yourself playing it along with the recording. Next, work on playing your own solos based on its chord progression, song form, and groove. Record your solos. Write down your favorite one and memorize it.

LISTEN **15** PLAY

SUMMARY

FORM	ARRANGEMENT	HARMONY	SCALE
12-BAR BLUES (1 CHORUS = 12 BARS)	INTRO: 4 M. 2 CHORUS MELODY 2 CHORUS SOLO 1 CHORUS MELODY END: 6 M.	D-7 G-7 A-7 A7	D BLUES

PLAY "I JUST WANNA BE WITH YOU" WITH YOUR OWN BAND!

"Leave Me Alone" is a *funk* tune. Funk has its roots in New Orleans street music. It started in the 1960s, and is a combination of rock, r&b, Motown, jazz, and blues. Funk has also influenced many rap artists. To hear more funk, listen to artists such as James Brown, Tower of Power, Kool and the Gang, the Meters, the Yellowjackets, Chaka Khan, Tina Turner, and the Red Hot Chili Peppers.

LESSON 13
TECHNIQUE/THEORY

Listen to "Leave Me Alone," and play along with the recording. Try to match the viola playing the melody.

LISTEN **18** P L A Y

ARTICULATION: LEGATO

Notes marked with legato [–] articulations in jazz and pop styles are played for their full rhythmic value. Legato marks are similar to slurs, but the articulations are marked on individual notes, rather than whole phrases. When you are *sustaining* (holding) a legato note, counting eighth notes as you play will help you to be sure it lasts for its full duration—all the way up to the rest.

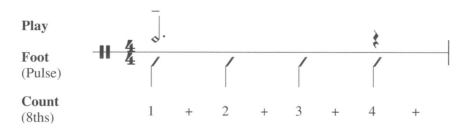

Practice playing notes legato along with the recording. Start and stop your notes as precisely as you can. Pay attention to the ends of notes as well as the beginnings.

Long, legato notes in a melody let listeners hear the rhythm section playing the groove. Short, staccato notes help the melody sound more like a part of the rhythm section. You can use a combination of both kinds of articulation.

Practice this articulation exercise with the recording.

LESSON 14
LEARNING THE GROOVE

HOOKING UP TO FUNK

LISTEN **18** PLAY

Listen to "Leave Me Alone." This funk groove has its roots in New Orleans street music—funky march music played on marching instruments (snare drums, bass drums, and so on) still found in the Mardi Gras parades each spring. Many New Orleans artists were important to the development of funk.

Funk rhythms are played with less of a swing feel than blues. There is an underlying sixteenth-note feel, similar to rock, so count "1 e + a, 2 e + a, 3 e + a, 4 e + a," as you play. In funk, the backbeat (beats 2 and 4) is especially accented, usually by the snare drum.

This exercise will help you hook up to funk. Play along with the recording, and match the viola. The music is written out below. Find the beat, and play the melody. It emphasizes the strong, funk backbeat.

LISTEN **20** PLAY

SYNCOPATIONS AND ARTICULATIONS

How you articulate syncopations changes how they feel in the groove. In this next example, each lick is played legato and then staccato. Each one has a unique sound. Echo each lick exactly as you hear it, focusing on articulations. You may find that they are easier to hear than to read, so listen carefully, and try to copy what you hear.

LESSON 15
IMPROVISATION

FORM AND ARRANGEMENT

Listen to "Leave Me Alone," and follow the form. This funk tune follows the 12-bar blues form.

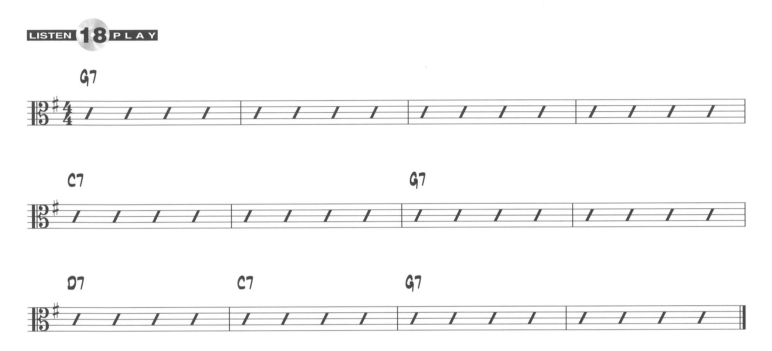

On the recording, the arrangement begins with a 4-measure introduction, featuring the rhythm section playing the groove.

IDEAS FOR IMPROVISING

Scales: G Blues

The G blues scale is a good choice for use with this tune. Play it on your viola.

Practice the notes of the G blues scale over a wider range.

CHORDS

The chords to "Leave Me Alone" are all the same type: dominant seventh chords, which you saw in chapter 2. These chords have the same sound, with the same *intervals*—the distances between pitches. The only change is that they are *transposed*; they begin on different notes. When you improvise, favor the chord tones of the symbol shown above the staff. This is called "making the changes," or interpreting the song's chords in your own way.

Practice the chord tones to "Leave Me Alone." Below each tone is an interval number showing the note's relationship to the chord root. Since all chords in this tune are dominant seventh chords, the interval numbers are the same: root, 3, 5, ♭7.

G7				C7				D7			
Root	3	5	♭7	Root	3	5	♭7	Root	3	5	♭7

RIFFS

Another good improvisation technique is to create a lick and then repeat it over and over. This repetition of a lick is called a *riff*. The lick's notes may come from a scale, from chord tones, from melody notes, or a combination of all three.

In the next exercise, we will play a riff built on this lick. Practice it until you can play it easily.

CALL AND RESPONSE

Echo each riff exactly as you hear it.

LISTEN **22** PLAY

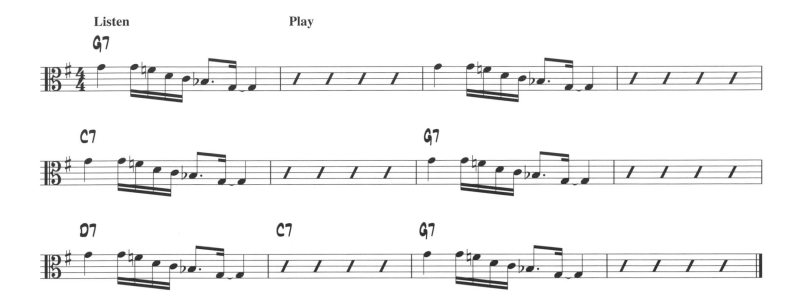

PERFORMANCE TIP

In blues, riffs work really well during a solo. They create musical tension, and the audience starts wondering how many times it will repeat before something new happens. The listeners move forward onto the edge of their seats, just waiting for a temporary conclusion—something that will relieve the musical tension and expectation that has been created.

WRITE YOUR OWN SINGLE RIFF SOLO

Create your own riff-based solo to "Leave Me Alone." Make sure the riff you create sounds good over all the chords. Write it out, and practice it along with the recording.

LISTEN **19** PLAY

TRANSPOSING LICKS

To make a single lick sound good over several different chords, you have to keep it simple and only use a couple of pitches. If you want to use a more complex lick, you can transpose it to different notes, similar to how the dominant seventh chords earlier were transposed to begin on different roots.

Practice this lick a few times until you can play it easily. Since it is based on the tune's first chord (G7), you can think of it as being in the "original" key. Interval numbers are shown below each note.

To transpose this lick, move its root to the root of each new chord (C7 and D7), and then use the same intervals to find the other notes. Practice the lick based on all three chords until you can play them easily.

CALL AND RESPONSE

Echo each riff exactly as you hear it.

WRITE YOUR OWN TRANSPOSING RIFF SOLO

Create your own riff-based solo to "Leave Me Alone." Transpose the same riff over all the chords. Write it out, and practice it along with the recording.

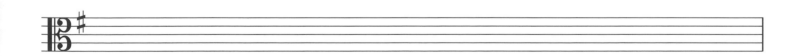

LESSON 16
READING

VIOLA PART

CUE NOTES   The small notes in measures 1 to 4 are *cue notes* showing the bass part (written out in treble clef). Read along with the bass notes to help you come in on time.

Play "Leave Me Alone" along with the recording, using the written viola part. If you can play in third position, try it up an octave.

LISTEN **19** PLAY

LEAVE ME ALONE
VIOLA PART

By Matt Marvuglio

LEAD SHEET

Play "Leave Me Alone," and follow along with the lead sheet. Create your own riff-based solo. Try transposing the licks by ear.

LEAVE ME ALONE

BY MATT MARVUGLIO

Memorizing your notes makes it easier to follow arrangement directions, such as "**D.S. AL CODA.**"

CHAPTER IV
DAILY PRACTICE ROUTINE

BENDING PITCHES

Raising or lowering the pitch of a note is often referred to as *"bending"* a note. Because bending notes on the viola is easy, violists tend to do it too much. Make sure that when you do it, you do it on purpose. Use it as an effect, like vibrato—not a constant.

Play a D on your viola for four beats at a medium-slow tempo. Play it straight, without bending the pitch.

Play the same note again. Begin the note normally, then try bending the pitch downwards.

Play the same note again, and after beginning the note normally, try bending the pitch upwards.

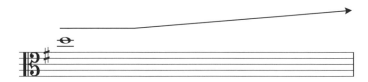

Bends are good effects when you are improvising. They will also help you play in tune.

BEND PRACTICE

Play along with the violin on the recording. Try to match its intonation exactly, starting and ending each note on pitch.

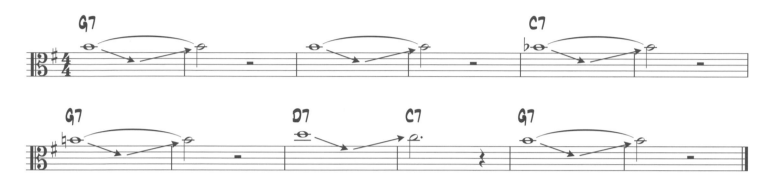

INTONATION/INTERVAL PRACTICE

This exercise will also help your intonation. Play this next track twice. First, play the top staff, then play the bottom staff. If you hear any "pulses" or "beats" between your note and the recording, it means that you are not playing in tune. Keep in tune with the track.

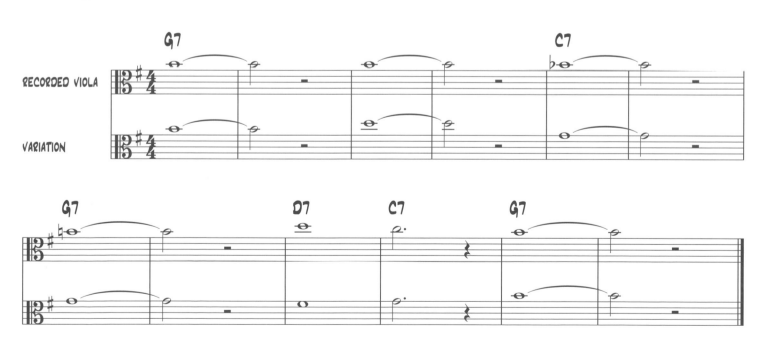

FUNK RHYTHMS

Practice this solo with the recording. Choose a combination of articulations to make your part groove with the rhythm section. Write your articulations into the score below.

LISTEN **19** PLAY

MAKING THE CHANGES

This solo draws its notes from three different sources. During **G7** measures, the notes come from the G blues scale. During the **C7** measures, the notes come from the chord tones of **C7**. During the **D7** measure, the notes come from chord tones of **D7**. Practice it alone first, and when you're ready, play it with the recording.

LISTEN **19** PLAY

PRACTICE TIP

The solo in the music above uses the same 1-measure rhythm over and over. If you learn that rhythm, the solo will become a lot easier to play.

SOLO PRACTICE

Practice the recorded viola solo to "Leave Me Alone." Before you play, read along with the recording (track 18), and finger the notes on viola without your bow. When you are ready, play along with the recording (track 19).

MEMORIZE

Create your own solo using any of the techniques you have learned, and write it out. Practice it, memorize it, and then record yourself playing the whole tune along with the recording.

SUMMARY

FORM	ARRANGEMENT	HARMONY	SCALE
12-BAR BLUES (1 CHORUS = 12 BARS)	INTRO: 4 M. 2 CHORUS MELODY 2 CHORUS SOLO 1 CHORUS MELODY	G7 C7 D7	G BLUES

PLAY "LEAVE ME ALONE" WITH YOUR OWN BAND!

"Affordable" is another funk tune, but it is lighter, with more of a feeling of open space. This style is popular with smooth-jazz artists. To hear more light funk, listen to artists such as David Sanborn, Earl Klugh, Walter Beasley, the Rippingtons, Dave Grusin, Kenny G, Bob James, and Anita Baker.

LESSON 17
TECHNIQUE/THEORY

Listen to "Affordable," and then play along with the recording. Try to match the viola in the melody.

LISTEN 25 PLAY

DYNAMICS

The melody of "Affordable" is made up mostly of long, drawn-out notes. The violist on the recording makes this melody more interesting by changing the notes' *dynamics*—their loudness and softness. In this tune, the last notes of each phrase generally *decrescendo* (gradually become softer). The notation for decrescendos is a wedge (sometimes called a *hairpin*) opening to the left (>). This shows where the sound should be louder (above the lines' widest point) and where it should be softer (above where the lines meet). The opposite of a decrescendo is a *crescendo* (gradually growing louder), which opens to the right (<).

Practice the melody to "Affordable" with the recording, and decrescendo at the end of phrases 1, 2, and 4. Notice how dynamics help to shape the melody. If you can play in third position, try this up an octave.

LISTEN **25** PLAY

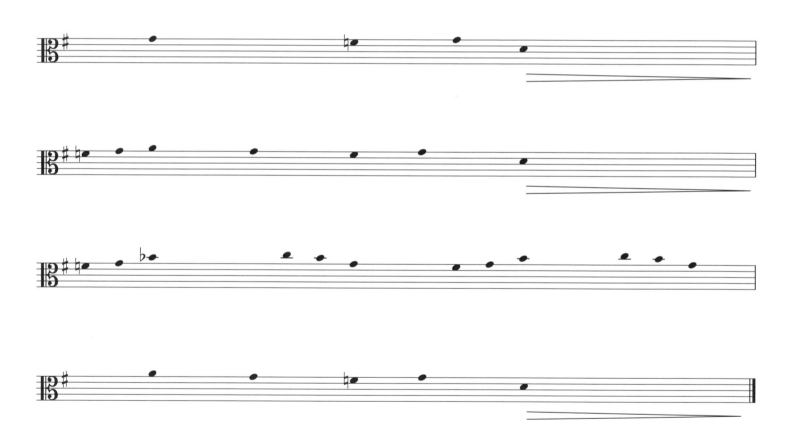

LESSON 18
LEARNING THE GROOVE

HOOKING UP TO LIGHT FUNK

LISTEN **25** PLAY

Listen to "Affordable." This groove is built around eighth notes, with some syncopated sixteenths in the B section. Notice that the band hooks up with the bass drum.

To learn this feel, practice counting sixteenths, leaving out the middle two sixteenths of each beat. Count out loud, along with a metronome or click track on the quarter-note pulse.

1 e + a 2 (e) (+) a 3 think think a 4   a 1   a 2   a 3   a 4   a

"Affordable" is a *light* funk tune. Like all funk music, eighth notes are played straight, not with a swing feel. The rhythm section plays fewer notes than they do in other styles of music. This makes the viola stand out even more than it does on the other tunes. What other elements of funk do you notice?

Listen to "Affordable." Find the pulse, and feel the sixteenth-note subdivisions. Notice that the backbeat is still emphasized, but it is lighter than it was in heavy funk.

VIOLA IN THE RHYTHM SECTION

To hook up to a groove, try playing the rhythm section's parts along with the recording. This viola line combines the bass, guitar, and keyboard parts. Feel the backbeat and the sixteenth notes as you play.

There are two different grooves in this tune. Play this first riff during phrases 1, 2, and 4, and at the introduction.

LISTEN **26** PLAY

Play this riff during phrase 3.

LISTEN **27** PLAY

LESSON 19
IMPROVISATION

FORM AND ARRANGEMENT

Listen to "Affordable," and follow the 16-bar form.

From practicing the rhythm section parts, you can tell that there are two primary musical ideas in this tune. When you play the melody, you can hear that there are two contrasting sections. Idea A is very sparse. It lasts for eight measures, with two phrases of viola melody. Idea B is in a more regular rhythm. It lasts for four measures. Then idea A returns for four measures. This form can be described as "AABA."

PRACTICE TIP

The 4-measure return of idea A at the end of the form may be confused with the eight measures of idea A that begin the new chorus. Altogether, there are twelve measures of this idea, so keep careful count.

Listen to the whole tune. Sing the melody while the viola plays the solo, and keep your place in the form. What is the arrangement on the recording? Is there an introduction or ending? Check your answer against the summary at the end of this chapter.

IDEAS FOR IMPROVISING

Scales: G Major and Minor Pentatonic Scales

The G major pentatonic scale will work well for improvising on this tune's A sections.

The G minor pentatonic scale will work well for improvising on this tune's B section.

CALL AND RESPONSE

1. Echo each phrase, exactly as you hear it.
2. Improvise an answer to each phrase. Imitate the sound and rhythmic feel of the phase you hear, and use the notes from the G pentatonic scales.

EMBELLISHING THE MELODY

The song melody is an excellent source of ideas for notes and licks. Whenever you play the melody, you contribute to the musical mood. The melody identifies the spirit and character of the song.

Think of the song melody as a compass. As you improvise, use it as your guide. Keep the melody at your solo's center, and improvise by adding or removing a few notes, or by varying their rhythm. Such changes are called *embellishments*.

Practice this embellished version of "Affordable." When you're ready, practice it along with the recording.

LISTEN 29 PLAY

Try playing the embellished version above "against" the original song melody. You can feel the added notes when you play them along with the original melody track.

Write out your own embellished version of the melody. Use the G pentatonic scales and the melody itself as sources for notes.

LISTEN **29** PLAY

Create a 1-chorus solo using any techniques you have learned. Memorize your solo, and practice it along with the recording.

LESSON 20
READING
VIOLA PART

VIOLA   Part label. The written parts you have been using were written specifically for viola. The key will also work for other instruments that read in C, or concert, such as keyboard or guitar. However, there may be some notation that will only make sense to a violist.

Play "Affordable" while reading the viola part, and solo where indicated. This part includes cue notes showing the rhythm section (bass and keyboard) parts. Use these cue notes to help you keep your place.

AFFORDABLE
VIOLA PART

By Matt Marvuglio

86

LEAD SHEET

Play "Affordable" while reading the lead sheet.

AFFORDABLE

BY MATT MARVUGLIO

"LIGHT FUNK" ♩ = 84

CHAPTER V
DAILY PRACTICE ROUTINE

VIBRATO

Another way to add interest to a melody (especially on notes of long duration) is to use *vibrato*. Vibrato is a slight, controlled vibration of a note's pitch, giving it a singing quality. In classical music, vibrato is used almost constantly. In the older popular styles, such as early jazz, vibrato is typically wide and rapid. In more contemporary popular styles, vibrato is generally used more sparingly, and with more variation in the speed and depth (variation of pitch) of vibrato. Many times, long notes begin straight, and then vibrato is added gradually. By listening to a lot of music, you will develop your own sense for when to use vibrato.

To add vibrato to a note, keep the center of your finger fixed on the fingerboard. Then roll your finger forward then back on the fingerboard around the center pitch, slightly raising and lowering the pitch. This is a technique where a teacher can be helpful. It is tricky.

There are several different styles of vibrato: finger, arm, and wrist. Practice them all, and try to get the most flexibility and variety out of your vibrato. That way, you'll have a wide palette of colors to use in your playing.

Practice long tones along with the recording. Start each note straight, then gradually add more and more vibrato to it, following the curvy line.

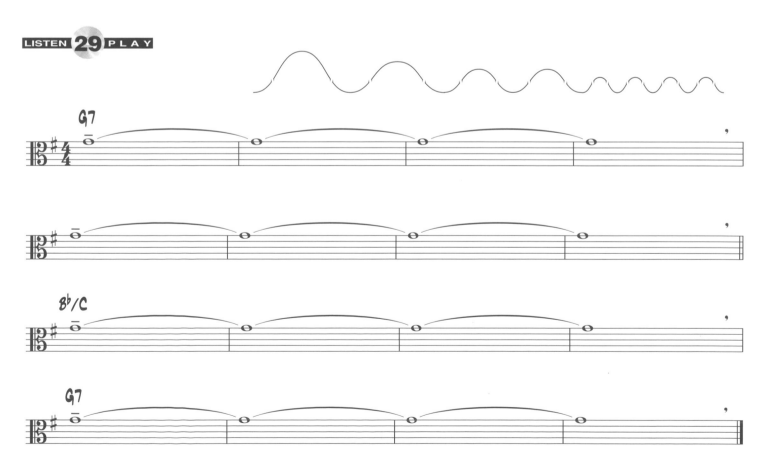

DYNAMICS AND VIBRATO

Try combining vibrato with dynamics, adding just a touch of vibrato at the end of phrases 1, 2, and 4. Don't overdo it! Just a little vibrato will sound great.

If you can play in second and third position, follow the fingerings shown. Using them will avoid open strings and allow you to use vibrato on those notes. If you're not ready for second and third position, then play the melody in first position, and try using your fourth finger instead of open strings to add a little vibrato.

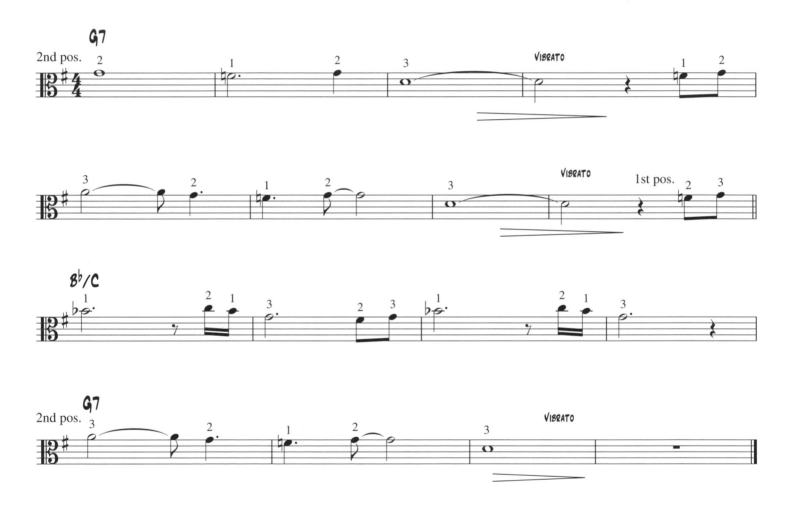

PENTATONIC SCALE PRACTICE

LISTEN **29** P L A Y

Create a solo using the tune's chords and notes of the G pentatonic scales, shown below the viola staff. Try using different rhythms that hook up to the light funk groove. Practice your solo with the recording.

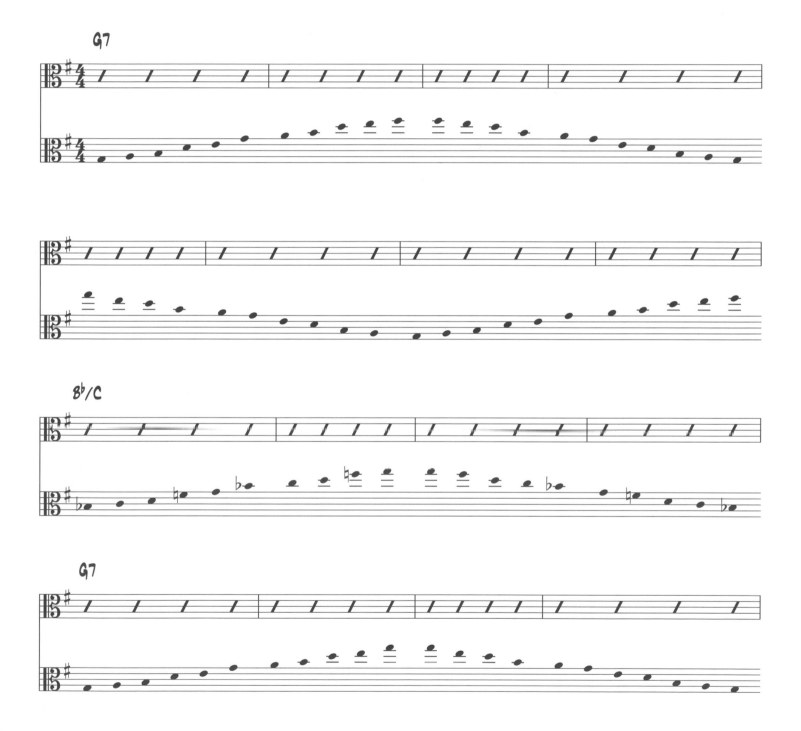

SOLO PRACTICE

Practice this solo along with the recording. Notice the use of the G pentatonic scales.

MEMORIZE

Create your own solo using any of the techniques you have learned, and write it out. Practice it, memorize it, and then record yourself playing the whole tune along with the CD.

SUMMARY

FORM
16-BAR AABA
(1 CHORUS = 16 BARS)
A: 4 M.
B: 4 M.

ARRANGEMENT
INTRO: 8 M.
1 CHORUS MELODY
1 CHORUS SOLO
1 CHORUS MELODY

HARMONY
A G7 B 8♭/C

SCALE
G MAJOR PENTATONIC   G MINOR PENTATONIC

PLAY "AFFORDABLE" WITH YOUR OWN BAND!

"Don't Look Down" is a *hard rock* tune. Hard rock first appeared in the late 1960s. It has characteristic heavy bass, long, drawn-out chords, and amplified instruments. To hear more hard rock, listen to artists such as Aerosmith, Metallica, Powerman 5000, the Allman Brothers Band, Rob Zombie, Godsmack, 311, Stone Temple Pilots, the Black Crowes, Steve Vai, and Smashing Pumpkins.

LESSON 21
TECHNIQUE/THEORY

LISTEN **30** PLAY

Listen to "Don't Look Down," and then play along with the recording. The viola and sax sometimes play in harmony, and the melody is doubled by the guitar. This tune has two different parts.

The first part has these four phrases.

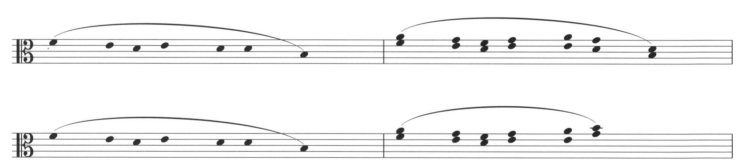

The second part has a riff that repeats four times.

It ends with the bass riff, played twice.

HARMONIZING A MELODY

If your band has two melodic instruments, such as two violas, or a viola and a sax, you might play the melody together and add some harmony.

The easiest way to add a harmony line is for one player to play thirds above or below the melody notes. This can be a little tricky, so follow your ear carefully. Some melody notes will sound better harmonized by a third above, some will sound better with a third below. If you are playing harmony, try to keep your harmony line smooth, and minimize the number of leaps you must take.

Notice the harmony lines in this tune. It lasts just a few notes and then returns to a unison melody. This is just one of many possibilities. How would you harmonize it? Try a few different ideas, and practice them along with the recording.

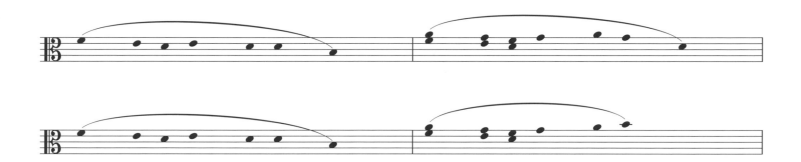

LESSON 22
LEARNING THE GROOVE

HOOKING UP TO HARD ROCK

Listen to "Don't Look Down." This tune has a standard rock/metal groove. It is a heavy feel, with very simple drum and bass parts. These parts must be simple because they are intended to be played in large arenas, where echoes would make busier parts sound muddy. It's a case of "less is more."

During the solos, the guitar doubles the bass, playing power chords in the second part. The keyboard plays sustained chords with an organ sound.

LISTEN **31** PLAY

Listen to the first part of "Don't Look Down." Chop along on the backbeats. Tap your foot on all four beats, and count out loud.

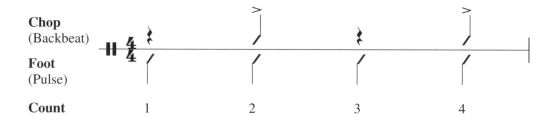

Try the same thing again. This time count the sixteenth notes out loud: 1e+a, 2e+a, 3e+a, 4e+a.

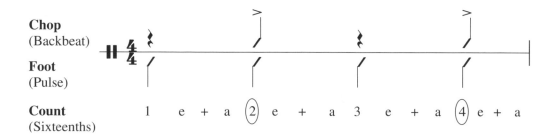

LEARNING "DON'T LOOK DOWN"

In the first part of this tune, the bass guitar plays a syncopated sixteenth-note riff. You hook up with that riff while you play the melody, and then you actually play the riff at the ending.

First, practice chopping the rhythm, or playing it on one note so that you can concentrate on the rhythm.

LISTEN **31** PLAY

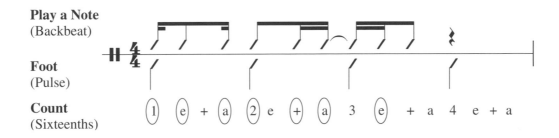

Next, play the actual notes. Hook up with the rhythm section. If you like, you can play this riff instead of the melody along with the A section of the full-band track.

LISTEN **31** PLAY

The second part of this tune also has a syncopated sixteenth-note figure. Practice playing the rhythms to this lick (also used at the Intro).

LISTEN **32** PLAY

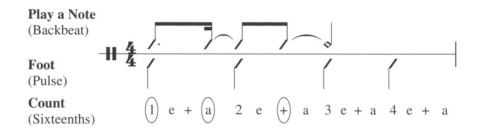

Practice the notes.

LISTEN **32** PLAY

Practice the whole tune along with the recording, and hook up with the rhythm section.

LISTEN **30** PLAY

LESSON 23
IMPROVISATION

FORM AND ARRANGEMENT

Listen to the recording and try to figure out the form and arrangement by ear. How long does each section of the form last? Is there an introduction or ending? For how many measures or beats does each chord last? Write down as much information as you can. Check your answers against the chord chart below and the summary at the end of this chapter.

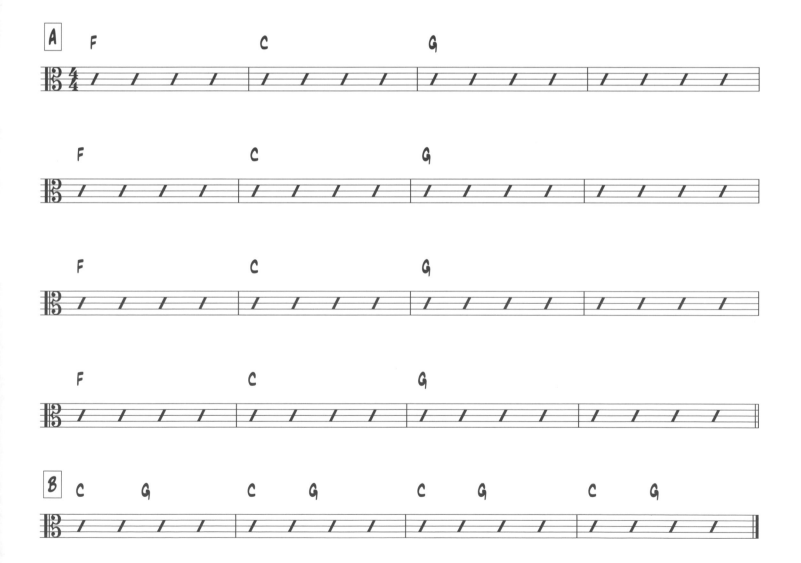

IDEAS FOR IMPROVISING

Scales: G Major and Minor Pentatonic Scales

The G major pentatonic scale will work well for improvising on this tune's A section.

The G minor pentatonic scale will work well for improvising on this tune's B section.

Practice both these scales. You can use both of them when you improvise, depending upon the chord.

CALL AND RESPONSE

Mixing Chord Tones and Pentatonic Scales

1. Echo the rhythm of each phrase exactly.
2. Improvise an answer to each phrase. Copy the rhythms of the recorded licks, but choose your own notes, based on the source indicated above the staff.

LISTEN **33** PLAY

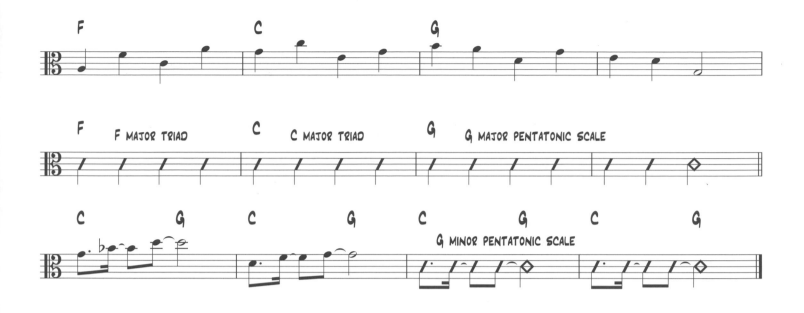

Write out a few of your own ideas.

LISTEN 34 PLAY

Create a 1-chorus solo using any techniques you have learned. Memorize your solo, and practice it with the recording.

LESSON 24
READING

VIOLA PART

 First and second ending markings. The first time you play these measures, play the *first ending*—the measures under the number 1. Then return to the begin-repeat sign (𝄆). The second time, skip the first ending and play the *second ending*—the measures under the number 2. Then, continue through the rest of the form.

Play "Don't Look Down" along with the recording. Use the written viola part.

LISTEN **34** PLAY

DON'T LOOK DOWN
VIOLA PART

BY MATT MARVUGLIO

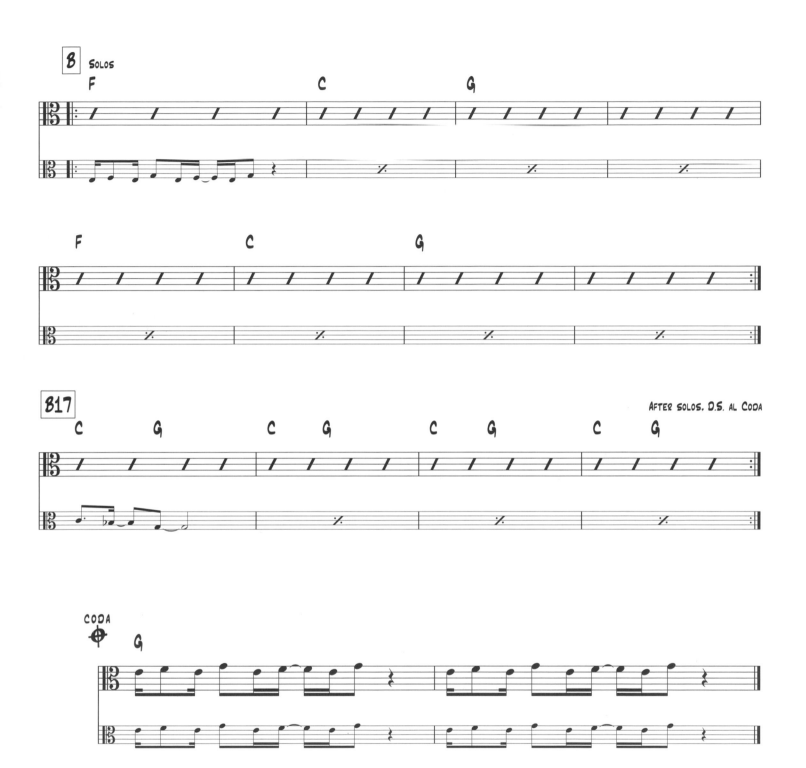

LEAD SHEET

Play your own part to "Don't Look Down," and follow along with the lead sheet.

LISTEN **34** PLAY

DON'T LOOK DOWN

By MATT MARVUGLIO

PRACTICE TIP

When you practice from a lead sheet, use it to help you keep your place. Even when you solo, follow the music as you play. This will help you to keep track of the form, so you can memorize it.

CHAPTER VI
DAILY PRACTICE ROUTINE

EMBELLISHMENT PRACTICE

Practice embellishing the melody to "Don't Look Down." Play the written 4-bar embellished melody and then your own 4-bar embellished melody. Include the original melody notes, on their original beats, in your embellished melody.

RHYTHM PRACTICE

This exercise will help you improve your ability to play steady sixteenth notes. Play any pitch or combination of pitches. Use a metronome, and start slow. Gradually increase the speed until you can play faster than the tempo on the recording (88 bpm). Then practice it along with the recording, using any pitch material we have studied. Simplify your pitches, if you need to. Focus on keeping steady time and articulating the accents.

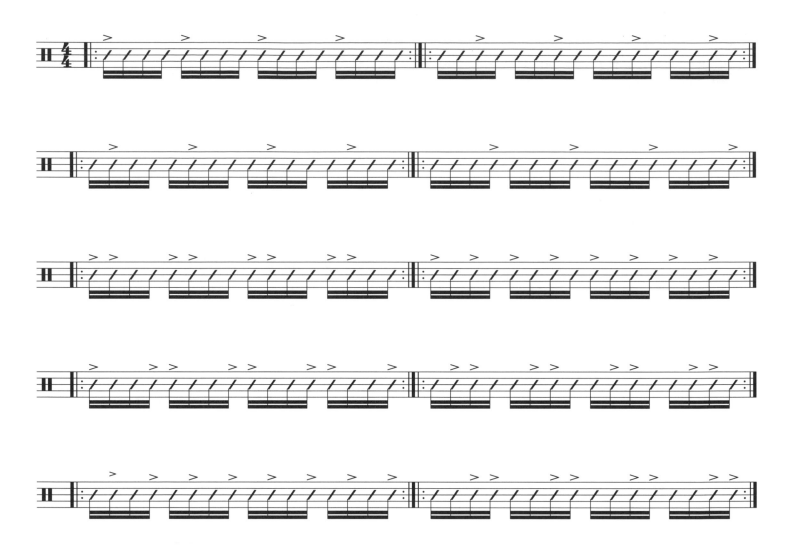

SOLO PRACTICE

Practice the recorded solo along with the CD.

LISTEN **34** PLAY

MEMORIZE

Create your own solo using any of the techniques you have learned, and write it out. Practice it, memorize it, and then record yourself playing the whole tune along with the recording.

LISTEN **34** PLAY

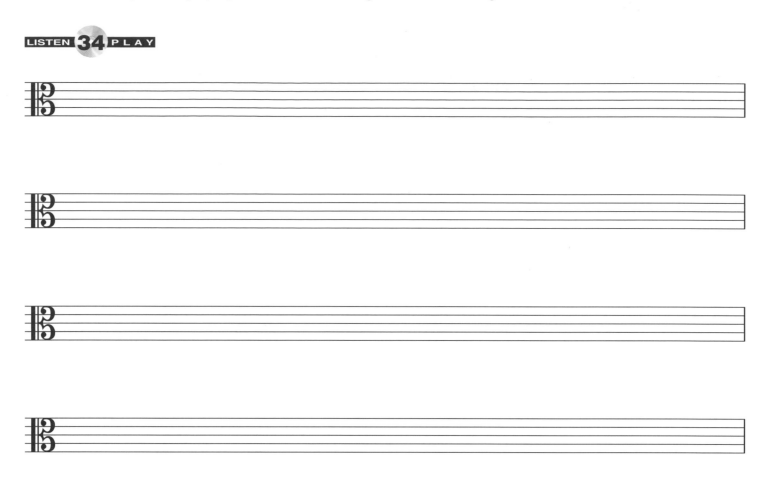

SUMMARY

FORM
20-BAR AB FORM
(1 CHORUS = 20 BARS)
A: 16 M.
B: 4 M.

ARRANGEMENT
INTRO: 4 M.
1 CHORUS MELODY
1 CHORUS SOLO
1 CHORUS MELODY
END: 2 M.

HARMONY

F   C   G

SCALE

G MAJOR PENTATONIC

G MINOR PENTATONIC

PLAY "DON'T LOOK DOWN" WITH YOUR OWN BAND!

PLAYING BOSSA NOVA   CHAPTER VII

"Take Your Time" is a *bossa nova* tune. Bossa nova began in Brazil,
combining American jazz and an Afro-Brazilian form of dance music called
samba. To hear more bossa nova, listen to Stan Getz, Antonio Carlos Jobim,
Eliane Elias, Astrud Gilberto, Flora Purim, Dave Valentine, and Spyro Gyra.

LESSON 25
TECHNIQUE/THEORY

Listen to "Take Your Time" on the recording. The melody is in two long phrases. Practice it along with the
recording, and try to match the viola.

LISTEN **35** P L A Y

This is the first phrase.

This is the second phrase.

FINGER PLACEMENT WITHIN A POSITION

Within a position, the placement of your fingers will often change depending on what you are playing. The melody to "Take Your Time" is a good example of this.

In the following exercise, notice how your fingers have to be in different places, even though the home note (tonic) is always D. Practicing different scales within a position helps you to play in tune.

Practice it along with the recording. Then play "Take Your Time" again, and feel how comfortable it is to make these different finger placements.

LESSON 26
LEARNING THE GROOVE

HOOKING UP TO BOSSA NOVA

Listen to "Take Your Time." This tune is a bossa nova, a style of music that originated in Brazil. Throughout the tune, a 2-bar rhythmic pattern repeats. This repeating pattern is an essential part of bossa nova. The drum plays it on a rim click.

Repeating rhythmic structures are at the heart of much African-based music, including Afro-Caribbean and most South and Latin American styles.

> ### PRACTICE TIP
>
> A good way to practice hooking up with a tune is to play all the other instruments' parts.

Listen to the drums on the recording and follow the drumbeat below. Drummers will occasionally vary the pattern slightly as they play through a song, but this is the basic beat to "Take Your Time." Notice that the snare drum (rim click) plays the repeating rhythmic pattern above.

Practice the bass drum part along with the recording. Match the bass drum rhythms exactly.

LISTEN 36 PLAY

The bass guitar rhythm is similar to the bass drum rhythm. It is a 2-bar rhythmic pattern that continues throughout the tune. Practice the bass guitar part along with the recording.

LISTEN 36 PLAY

Play the snare drum rhythms, which sound the bossa nova pattern you saw at the beginning of this lesson. Hook up with the bossa nova groove.

LISTEN 36 PLAY

Play the keyboard's own 2-bar rhythm. You will be playing the top note of each keyboard chord. Match the keyboard on the recording. You may prefer to play this up an octave.

LISTEN 36 PLAY

CHALLENGE

Try to figure out the guitar part by ear.

LESSON 27
IMPROVISATION

FORM AND ARRANGEMENT

Listen to "Take Your Time," and try to figure out the form by ear. Check your answers with the chord chart and summary. Then continue with this chapter.

LISTEN **35** PLAY

D-7

EᵇMAJ7

DMAJ7

IDEAS FOR IMPROVISING

Scales: D Pentatonic Scales

For the first twelve measures of this tune (over the **D–7** and **E♭MA7** chords), we will use the D minor pentatonic scale to improvise. Practice this scale on your viola.

Practice the D minor pentatonic scale throughout your entire range.

In the last four measures (over the **DMA7** chord), solo using notes from the D major pentatonic scale. Major pentatonic scales work well when improvising on major or major seventh chords. Practice this scale on your viola.

Practice the D major pentatonic scale throughout your entire range.

CALL AND RESPONSE

1. Echo each phrase, exactly as you hear it.

2. Improvise an answer to each phrase. Imitate the sound and rhythmic feel of the phrase you hear, and use the notes from the D pentatonic scales.

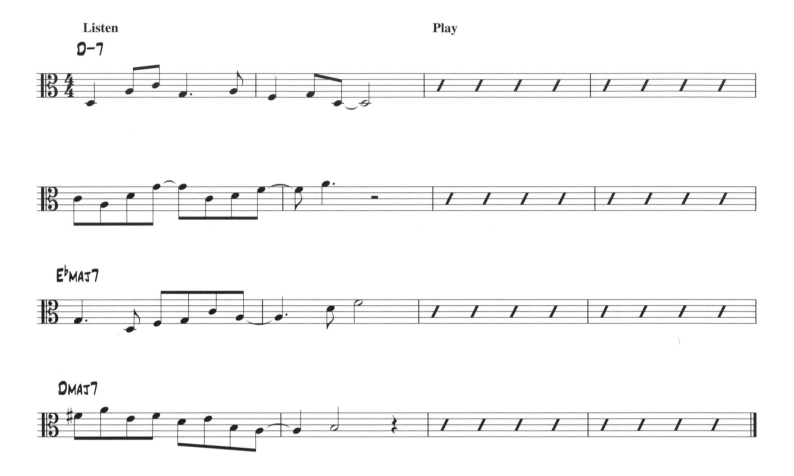

Write out some of your own ideas. Use notes from the D pentatonic scales.

LISTEN **36** PLAY

Create a 1-chorus solo using any techniques you have learned. Memorize your solo, practice it along with the recording, and then record it.

LESSON 28
READING

VIOLA PART

 Two-measure repeat. Repeat the previously notated two measures.

Play "Take Your Time," and use the written part. Alternatively, you could play the bass line or the keyboard line. Use the full band track (track 35), if you do.

LISTEN **36** PLAY

TAKE YOUR TIME
VIOLA PART

By Matt Marvuglio

LEAD SHEET

Play "Take Your Time," and follow the lead sheet.

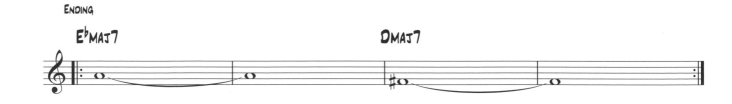

TAKE YOUR TIME

By Matt Marvuglio

"Bossa" ♩ = 126

CHAPTER VII
DAILY PRACTICE ROUTINE

CHORD TONES AND TENSIONS

A *tension* note is an extension of a chord. The example below shows extended chord arpeggios. They are another good source of notes to use in your solos. Tensions are marked with a T below.

Call and Response

1. Echo each phrase, exactly as you hear it. Notice the use of tensions.
2. Improvise an answer to each phrase. Imitate the sound and rhythmic feel of the phrase you hear, and use chord tones. Try using the same tension notes as you hear on the recording.

Write out some of your own ideas. Use notes from the D pentatonic scales and from the chord tones and tensions of D–7, E♭MA♫7, and DMA♫7.

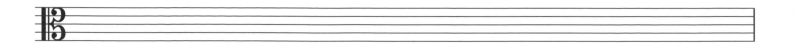

LEARNING NEW SCALES

Chord tones and tensions are good sources for notes in your improvisations, as are scales. The pentatonic and the blues scales are great sources of ideas. There are many other scales that are also good sources of ideas. As you get comfortable with the chords and scales you know, you may wish to explore some new ones.

Learn to play any new scale using the same approach that you used to learn the simpler ones.

1. One octave. Play the scale in just one octave, up and down, so that you can focus on what the pitches are.
2. Full range. Practice it throughout the whole range of your viola, as low and as high as you can go.
3. Rhythmic and melodic figures. Practice it in rhythm, against a metronome or a recording, making up little melodic and rhythmic figures using the notes from the scale, similar to the exercises you've been doing in this book.
4. Write a solo. Write out a solo that uses the new scale(s).

Once you get a new scale under your fingers, you will be able to use it musically. Writing out some melodies based on your new sources of notes is a great way to help you master them. Try to use all these techniques with the following three scales that can be used with "Take Your Time."

The D Dorian scale (or "mode") will work well over the **D-7** chords of "Take Your Time."

The D Phrygian scale will work well over the **E♭MAJ7** chords.

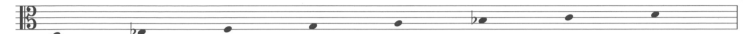

The D major scale will work well over the **DMAJ7** chords.

Practice these scales using the above approach. Make sure to adjust your finger placement, as shown in lesson 25. When you go from the major scale to Dorian, lower your second finger a half step. And then when you go from there to Phrygian, lower your first finger a half step. Practice lowering and raising your fingers by half steps; it will help you play many kinds of tunes.

As you practice new scales or other sources of ideas, concentrate on each note you play, listen carefully, and adjust your fingers to match your ear.

SOLO PRACTICE

Practice the recorded solo along with the recording. Notice the use of long tones, chord tones, and tensions.
What scales seem to be used?

MEMORIZE

Create your own solo using any of the techniques you have learned, and write it out. Practice it, memorize it, and then record yourself playing the whole tune along with the recording.

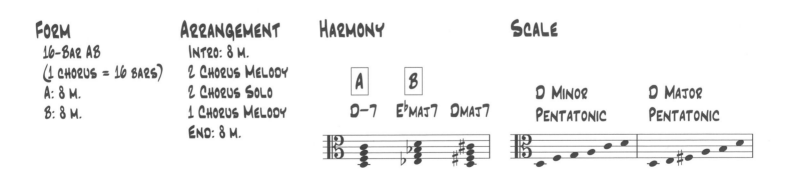

SUMMARY

FORM
16-BAR AB
(1 CHORUS = 16 BARS)
A: 8 M.
B: 8 M.

ARRANGEMENT
INTRO: 8 M.
2 CHORUS MELODY
2 CHORUS SOLO
1 CHORUS MELODY
END: 8 M.

HARMONY

A	B
D-7	E♭MAJ7 DMAJ7

SCALE

D MINOR PENTATONIC

D MAJOR PENTATONIC

PLAY "TAKE YOUR TIME" WITH YOUR OWN BAND!

PLAYING STOP TIME

"Stop It" is a blues/jazz tune in which *stop time* accents the melody, like a question and answer. Stop-time is very common in blues, jazz, and other styles. To hear more stop-time blues, listen to artists such as Miles Davis, John Coltrane, Jim Hall, Sarah Vaughn, Bill Evans, Ella Fitzgerald, Louis Armstrong, Abbie Lincoln, Dizzy Gillespie, and Charlie Parker.

LESSON 29
TECHNIQUE/THEORY

Listen to the recording and then play along with the melody. Try to match the viola. Notice that there are only three different licks.

LISTEN **39** PLAY

ARTICULATION

A way to make this melody come alive is by using different articulations for the licks. The first, third, and fifth lick should all be played legato, with the notes sounding connected to each other. This is often marked with a slur. Only the first note should be articulated.

The second lick (repeated after licks 3 and 5) is made up of five notes with alternating short accents (swing staccato) and legato articulations.

The lick at bar 9 is also legato.

Practice the melody along with the recording, articulating these licks as shown above.

LISTEN **40** PLAY

LESSON 30
LEARNING THE GROOVE

HOOKING UP TO STOP-TIME BLUES

Listen to "Stop It." This jazz cymbal beat is at the heart of jazz rhythm. The "spang spang a-lang" cymbal beat is unique to jazz, and it has been its primary pattern since the 1940s. Its underlying pulse is the same as the shuffle. This pattern has accompanied Count Basie, Miles Davis, John Coltrane, Duke Ellington, and thousands of other jazz artists.

LISTEN **39** PLAY

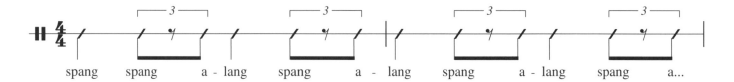

spang   spang   a - lang   spang   a - lang   spang   a - lang   spang   a...

STOP TIME

In stop time, the groove is punctuated by *stop-time kicks*. These are rhythmic figures, usually just one or two beats long, that punctuate the melody. That is why it is called "stop time"—the rhythm section "stops" or rests.

Play the melody along with the recording, and match the viola part. On this tune, the viola plays the melody during the stop-time sections. Tap the pulse with your foot, and feel the subdivisions. Hook up with the groove.

LISTEN **40** PLAY

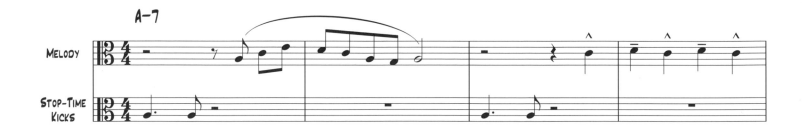

REGULAR TIME

During the solos, the rhythm section *plays time*. The drums play a steady beat, the bass *walks* (plays steady quarter notes), and the keyboard and guitar play chords.

The guitar plays chords in a 2-measure pattern. Play the guitar part (the top notes of its chords) along with the recording. Match the guitar's articulation and time feel. You might prefer to play this up an octave.

The keyboard also has a repeating 2-measure pattern. Play the keyboard part (the top notes of its chords) along with the recording. Match the keyboard's articulation and time feel, and notice how it hooks up with the guitar part. You might prefer to play this up an octave.

LESSON 31
IMPROVISATION

FORM AND ARRANGEMENT

Listen to "Stop It," and try to figure out the form and arrangement by ear. Check your answer against the summary at the end of this chapter.

LISTEN **39** PLAY

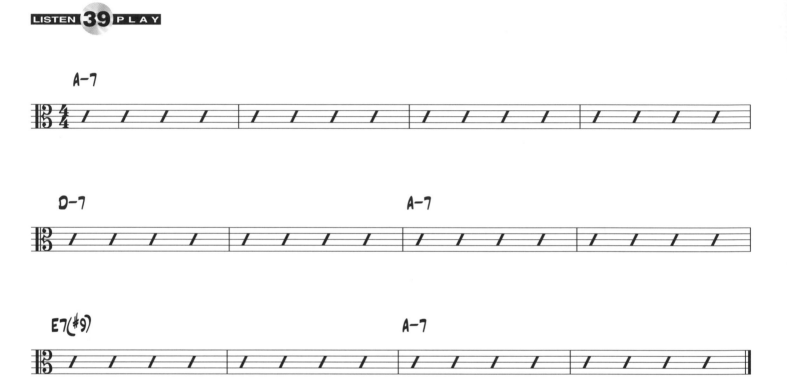

IDEAS FOR IMPROVISING

Scales: A Blues

Use the A blues scale to improvise over this tune.

Practice the notes of the A blues scale throughout the entire range of your viola.

Practice playing the chord tones used in this tune. Notice the extension of the **E7(♯9)** chord.

The **E7(♯9)** chord has a dissonance between the G-natural and the G-sharp. This color is one of the defining elements of the chord progression, and will lend a distinctive color to your solo. Here is an example of the kind of lick you can play that makes use of that dissonance.

CALL AND RESPONSE

1. Echo each phrase, exactly as you hear it.
2. Improvise an answer to each phrase. Imitate the sound and rhythmic feel of the phrase you hear. Use the A blues scale, chord tones, and tensions.

LISTEN **42** PLAY

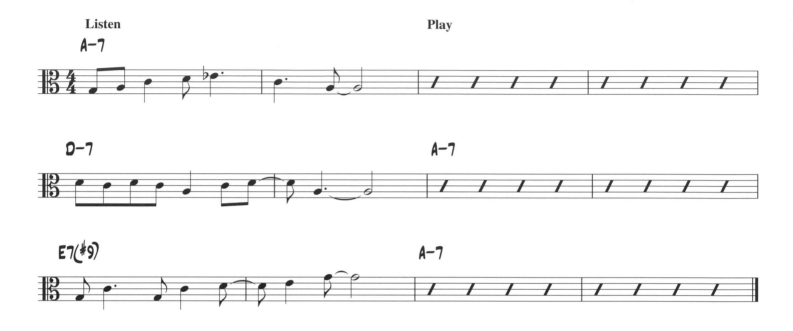

LISTEN **43** PLAY

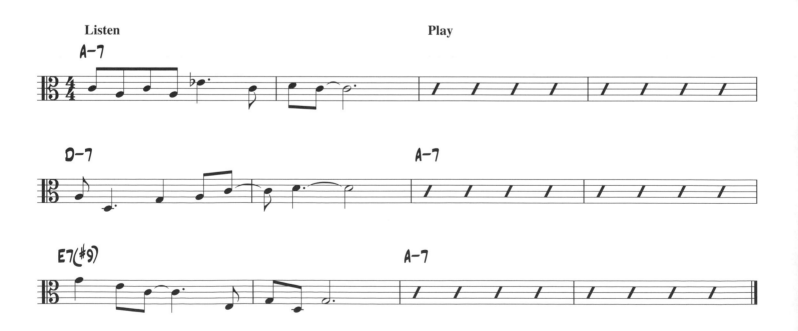

Write out some of your own ideas. Use chord tones and notes from the A blues scale.

LISTEN 44 P L A Y

Create a 2-chorus solo using any techniques you have learned. Memorize your solo, and practice it along with the recording.

LESSON 32
READING

VIOLA PART

D.C. AL CODA From the beginning, and take the coda. Jump to the very first measure of the tune, and play from there. When you reach the first coda symbol, skip ahead to the next coda symbol (at the end). This is similar to the "**D.S. AL CODA**," but instead of going to a sign, go to the first measure of the tune.

Play "Stop It" along with the recording, and read from the written viola part.

LISTEN **44** PLAY

STOP IT
VIOLA PART

By Matt Marvuglio

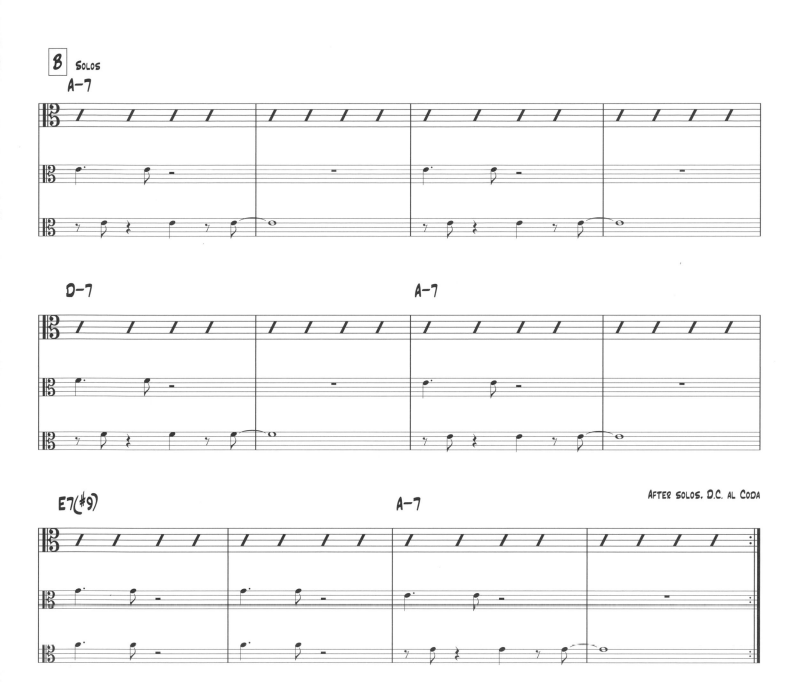

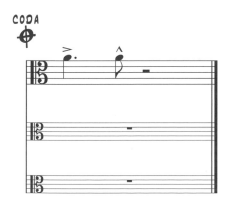

LEAD SHEET

Play "Stop It" from the lead sheet.

STOP IT

By Matt Marvuglio

CHAPTER VIII
DAILY PRACTICE ROUTINE

SCALE PRACTICE

As you become comfortable with all the different scales and chords, you will find it easier to use them. Practice them every day as part of your routine. You will learn them thoroughly, and your general technique, facility, and stamina will also improve as a result.

Here are some more strategies for practicing scales.

1. **Practice scales in all twelve keys.** Begin with the key of a tune that you are working on. For "Stop It," we're in the key of A minor, so if you were practicing minor scales, you might begin by practicing the A minor scale. Then move the scale up a fifth (or down a fourth), and practice the E minor scale. Then the B minor scale. Keep moving the scale up a fifth (or down a fourth) until you are back at the key of A minor. This is called the "circle of fifths."

Continue…

Some scales are easier on the viola and some are more difficult. The keys of D and A are relatively easy, while the keys of D♭ and F# are relatively difficult. Practice slowly, and listen to make sure that you are in tune. With practice, you'll get used to all of them. The notes in all the major scales have the same relationships to each other, so as you get used to these relationships, generally, they will all become easier to play.

2. **Practice scales in thirds.** Play the scale, but skip every other note. For A minor, you'd play A, C, B, D, C, E, D, F…. When the range gets too high, drop back down to your lowest octave, and pick up where you left off. Try this in all twelve keys.

Continue…

3. **Practice scales in triads.** Starting from the tonic note, play a triad using only scale tones. Then play a triad from the second note. This will help show you what triads are a natural part of the scale, and all kinds of chords will begin to fall naturally under your fingers. (These are called *diatonically occurring triads.*) Try this in all twelve keys.

Continue…

4. **Practice scales in seventh chords.** This is like practicing scales in triads, but you play four notes in each series: A, C♯, E, G♯; B, D, F♯, A; C♯, E, G♯, B….

Continue…

5. **Try different variations.** Invent your own similar exercises, such as trying different permutations (variations, or different orders) of each of the above exercises, or from any other source. For example, a variation of scales in thirds would be to first play a scale going upward in thirds, but then play the next scale in the circle of fifths going downward in thirds, alternating directions each time.

Continue…

Or start the exercises by playing thirds going downward.

Continue…

6. **Practice scales over tunes.** Decide what scales you will use over each chord, and then practice soloing along with a recording, using the right scale exercise over the right chord. In this example, you can see how the A minor was used at the beginning of the solo, then it switches to D blues, and then to A blues.

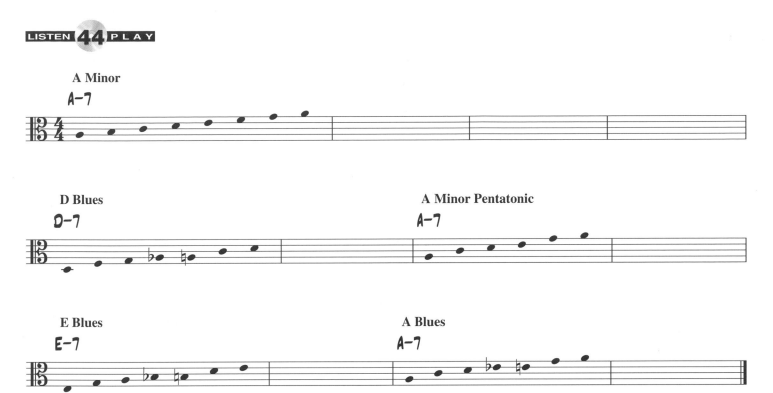

CHORD TONE PRACTICE

Practicing the chord tones of tunes is good for your technique because it involves big interval jumps and challenging string crossings. When practicing chord tones for technique, watch your bow carefully, and make sure you're only hitting one string at a time. Try to plan your fingering for more than one note at a time. That way, your fingers will get to a note before your bow does.

Practice this melody, which uses chord tones and tensions of the chords to "Stop It."

LISTEN **44** P L A Y

CALL AND RESPONSE

1. Echo each phrase, exactly as you hear it.
2. Improvise an answer to each phrase. Use the rhythms shown and choose notes from the chord tones shown below the staff. Be sure to mix up the chord tones, rather than playing them in the order shown.

LISTEN **45** P L A Y

Write out a few of your own ideas. Use chord tones and the A blues scale.

Create a 2-chorus solo using any techniques you have learned. Memorize your solo, and practice it along with the recording.

SOLO PRACTICE

Practice the recorded viola solo (from track 39) along with the CD.

MEMORIZE

Create your own solo using any of the techniques you have learned, and write it out. Practice it, memorize it, and then record yourself playing the whole tune along with the recording.

LISTEN **44** PLAY

SUMMARY

FORM	ARRANGEMENT	HARMONY	SCALE
12-BAR BLUES (1 CHORUS = 12 BARS)	2 CHORUS MELODY 4 CHORUS SOLO 2 CHORUS MELODY END: 1 M.	A–7 D–7 E7(#9)	A BLUES

PLAY "STOP IT" WITH YOUR OWN BAND!

FINAL REMARKS

Congratulations on completing the *Berklee Practice Method*. You now have a good idea of the role of the viola in a band, and have command of the eight grooves/time feels of these tunes. The melodies and harmonic progressions that you have learned are important and useful parts of your musical vocabulary. In addition, you have tools and ideas for creating your own parts and solos. This is a great start!

What to do next? Play along with your favorite recordings. Find records that you hear other musicians talking about. Learn these tunes, grooves, and parts. There is a good reason that musicians talk about certain bands, albums, or violists. Continue your theory, reading, and technique work. Investigate chord scales and modes. Learn all your key signatures (major and minor), scales, and chord arpeggios.

Develop your concept of what it means to play viola. Realize how important you are as a violist in a band. You have a big responsibility, taking care of the melody, the harmony, and the groove. It is a powerful position.

Play your viola every day, by yourself and with others, and get the sound in your body.

Keep the beat!

—Matt and Mimi

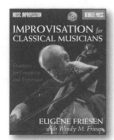

More Fine Publications from Berklee Press

GUITAR

BERKLEE BASIC GUITAR
by William Leavitt
50449460 Phase 1 Book.................................. $9.99
50449470 Phase 2 Book.................................. $9.95

BERKLEE BLUES GUITAR SONGBOOK
by Michael Williams
50449593 Book/CD.................................. $24.99

BERKLEE GUITAR CHORD DICTIONARY
by Rick Peckham
50449546 Jazz.................................. $10.99
50449596 Rock.................................. $12.99

THE CHORD FACTORY
by Jon Damian
50449541 .... $24.95

CLASSICAL STUDIES FOR PICK-STYLE GUITAR
by William Leavitt
50449440 Volume 1: Book.................................. $10.99

CREATIVE CHORDAL HARMONY FOR GUITAR
by Mick Goodrick and Tim Miller
50449613 Book/CD.................................. $19.99

FUNK/R&B GUITAR
by Thaddeus Hogarth
50449569 Book/CD.................................. $19.95

JAZZ IMPROVISATION FOR GUITAR
by Garrison Fewell
A Harmonic Approach
50449594 Book/CD $24.99
A Melodic Approach
50449503 Book/CD Pack.................................. $24.99

MELODIC RHYTHMS FOR GUITAR
by William Leavitt
50449450 .... $14.95

A MODERN METHOD FOR GUITAR
by William Leavitt
Volume 1: Beginner
50449400 Book $14.95
50449404 Book/CD.................................. $22.95
50448066 DVD-ROM.................................. $29.95
50448065 Book/DVD-ROM $34.99
Volume 2: Intermediate
50449410 Book.................................. $14.95
Volume 3: Advanced
50449420 Book.................................. $16.95
1, 2, 3 Complete
50449468 Book.................................. $34.95
Jazz Songbook, Vol. 1
50449539 Book/CD.................................. $14.99
Rock Songbook
50449624 Book/CD.................................. $17.99

Berklee Press Publications feature material developed at the Berklee College of Music. To browse the complete Berklee Press Catalog, go to
www.berkleepress.com

PLAYING THE CHANGES: GUITAR
by Mitch Seidman and Paul Del Nero
50449509 Book/CD.................................. $19.95

THE PRACTICAL JAZZ GUITARIST
by Mark White
50449618 Book/CD.................................. $19.99

READING STUDIES FOR GUITAR
by William Leavitt
50449490 Book $16.99

BASS

BASS LINES
by Joe Santerre
50449542 Fingerstyle Funk: Book/CD $19.95
50449478 Rock: Book/CD $19.95

CHORD STUDIES FOR ELECTRIC BASS
by Rich Appleman
50449750 Book $16.99

FUNK BASS FILLS
by Anthony Vitti
50449608 Book/CD.................................. $19.99

INSTANT BASS
by Danny Morris
50449502 Book/CD.................................. $14.95

READING CONTEMPORARY ELECTRIC BASS
by Rich Appleman
50449770 Book $19.95

DRUMS

BEGINNING DJEMBE
by Michael Markus & Joe Galeota
50449639 DVD.................................. $14.99

CREATIVE JAZZ IMPROVISATION FOR DRUM SET
featuring Yoron Israel
50449549 DVD.................................. $24.95

DRUM SET WARM-UPS
by Rod Morgenstein
50449465 Book $12.99

DRUM STUDIES
by Dave Vose
50449617 Book $12.99

EIGHT ESSENTIALS OF DRUMMING
by Ron Savage
50448048 Book/CD.................................. $19.99

NEW WORLD DRUMMING
by Pablo Peña "Pablitodrum"
50449547 DVD.................................. $24.95

TURNTABLE TECHNIQUE – 2ND EDITION
by Stephen Webber
50449482 Book/2-Record Set.................................. $34.99

WORLD JAZZ DRUMMING
by Mark Walker
50449568 Book/CD $22.99

KEYBOARD

BERKLEE JAZZ KEYBOARD HARMONY
by Suzanna Sifter
50449606 Book/CD.................................. $24.99

BERKLEE JAZZ PIANO
by Ray Santisi
50448047 Book/CD.................................. $19.99

CHORD-SCALE IMPROVISATION FOR KEYBOARD
by Ross Ramsay
50449597 Book/CD Pack.................................. $19.99

CONTEMPORARY PIANO TECHNIQUE
by Stephany Tiernan
50449545 Book/DVD.................................. $29.99

HAMMOND ORGAN COMPLETE
by Dave Limina
50449479 Book/CD.................................. $24.99

JAZZ PIANO COMPING
by Suzanne Davis
50449614 Book/CD.................................. $19.99

PIANO ESSENTIALS
by Ross Ramsay
50448046 Book/CD.................................. $24.99

SOLO JAZZ PIANO
by Neil Olmstead
50449444 Book/CD.................................. $39.95

VOICE

THE CONTEMPORARY SINGER – 2ND EDITION
by Anne Peckham
50449595 Book/CD.................................. $24.99

SINGER'S HANDBOOK
by Anne Peckham
50448053 Book $9.95

TIPS FOR SINGERS
by Carolyn Wilkins
50449557 Book/CD.................................. $19.95

THE ULTIMATE PRACTICE GUIDE FOR VOCALISTS
with Donna McElroy
50448017 DVD.................................. $19.95

VOCAL TECHNIQUE
featuring Anne Peckham
50448038 DVD.................................. $19.95

VOCAL WORKOUTS FOR THE CONTEMPORARY SINGER
by Anne Peckham
50448044 Book/CD.................................. $24.95

YOUR SINGING VOICE
by Jeannie Gagné
50449619 Book/CD.................................. $29.99

INTRODUCTION

This manual is one of a series now being published, primarily for U.S. Army Special Forces, that deals with subjects pertaining to destructive techniques and their applications to targets in guerrilla and unconventional warfare. The series consists of both classified and unclassified manuals of three types:

a. Unconventional Warfare Reference Manuals consist of detailed, illustrated abstracts of the technical literature. They are designed to provide sources of information and ideas and to minimize duplication of effort.

b. Unconventional Warfare Devices and Technique Manuals cover incendiaries, explosives, weapons, and harmful additives. They present principles of construction and methods of use of devices and techniques that are proven reliable and effective.

c. Unconventional Warfare Target Manuals identify critical components of selected targets and describe methods for destruction of the target using applicable devices and techniques.

This manual on incendiaries is written to serve the U.S. Army Special Forces in the field. It covers all aspects of incendiary systems including the incendiary devices, means for igniting them, techniques for their use, methods of improvising them, and sources of material supply. Some of the devices can be improvised from locally available materials. Detailed instructions are given for preparation steps. Others can be improvised if more sophisticated materials are obtainable. Still others require fabrication or formulation in a laboratory or industrial plant.

All of the devices and techniques herein reported are known to work. It is a special feature of this manual to present only those items that produce useful results as verified by independent test. Before an item becomes eligible for inclusion in this manual, it passes engineering tests designed to evaluate effectiveness, reliability, and safety. Not only does this program provide performance data, it also eliminates items that prove to be ineffective, unreliable, or unsafe, even though they may exist in print elsewhere. Although laboratory and final testing are adequate, user familiarization with construction, operation, and performance of each item or technique is recommended before tactical use. Instructions and formulations must be followed precisely to assure proper functioning of the incendiaries.

The material in this manual is grouped into six chapters.

Each chapter is subdivided into paragraphs having 4-digit numbers, the first representing section numbers, and the last two paragraph numbers.

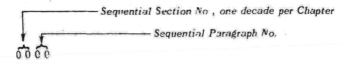

This numbering system was selected to make location of material convenient for the reader, once he has become familiar with the arrangement. Section numbers are uniquely assigned to one subject and repeated for the same subject in other manuals of this series. Also for convenience, each paragraph (except in *Introduction*) is subdivided uniformly into four subparagraphs:

Description, Material and Equipment, Preparation, and Application.

It is anticipated that this manual will be revised or changed from time to time. In this way it will be possible to update present material and add new devices and techniques as they become available. Comments are invited and the submission of new information is encouraged. Address information to Commanding Officer, U.S. Army Frankford Arsenal, SMUFA-U3200, Philadelphia, Pa., 19137.

TM 31-201-1

TECHNICAL MANUAL }
No. 31-201-1 }

HEADQUARTERS
DEPARTMENT OF THE ARMY
WASHINGTON, D.C., *20 May 1966*

Unconventional Warfare Devices and Techniques

INCENDIARIES

CHAPTER 1
INTRODUCTION

0001. INCENDIARY SYSTEMS

a. This manual covers all aspects of incendiary systems. It describes useful initiators, igniters, incendiary materials, delay mechanisms, and spontaneous combustion devices designed for direct use in sabotage and unconventional warfare.

b. Incendiaries are primarily used in sabotage to set fire to wooden structures and other combustible targets. Certain incendiaries, such as thermite, can be used for melting, cutting, or welding metals.

c. The most basic incendiary system consists of putting a lighted match to an easily combustible material. However, a simple match is not always effective. There are many important combustible targets that require far more heat for reliable ignition than is available from a match. There are also instances where delayed ignition is essential for sabotage success. This manual contains formulations and devices to satisfy the requirements for high ignition heat and predetermined ignition delay times for use in sabotage and other harassment actions.

d. Every incendiary system consists of a group of elements starting with an initiator and ending with the main incendiary material. If the initiator does not produce enough heat for reliable ignition of the combustible target, an intermediate or booster incendiary is required. More than one booster is necessary for some targets. The initiator (ch 2) can consist of a simple match, a match and a fuse cord, an acid, or water. The intermediate heat sources are generally called igniters (ch 3). Igniters produce sufficient heat to set the principal incendiary charge (ch 4) aflame. Delay mechanisms (ch 5) are frequently used to prevent detection of the saboteur by postponement of the fire for some limited, predetermined time after placement and actuation of the device.

e. Spontaneous combuston is a good sabotage tool. Favorable conditions can be established for the deliberate employment of spontaneous combustion (ch 6), that is, setting combustible material aflame without application of direct flame or spark.

f. All of the devices and techniques described herein have been thoroughly checked by independent test to make certain that they work as intended. Detailed instructions are given for the necessary ingredients and their preparation. It is important that these instructions be followed carefully to be sure that the devices will operate properly. In addition, close attention to the instructions will assure safety.

0002. DEFINITIONS

Common terms used in connection with incendiary systems are defined below. Note that the definitions are worded so as to cover only incendiaries. Some of the terms have additional meanings in the related field of explosives.

a. Delay Mechanism. Chemical, electrical, or mechanical elements that provide a time delay. Elements may be used singly or in combination. They provide a

4

predetermined, limited time interval before an incendiary starts to burn.

b. Fuse. A flexible fabric tube containing powder that is used to start fires at some remote location. The powder in the fuse burns and provides a time delay.

c. Igniter. An intermediate charge between an initiator and an incendiary material. It is set aflame by the initiator and produces sufficient heat at high temperature to ignite the main incendiary. Igniters are fast burning and relatively short lived.

d. Incendiary Material. A material that burns with a hot flame for long periods. Its purpose is to set fire to wooden structures and other combustible targets.

e. Incendiary System. A group of elements that are assembled to start fires. The system consists of initiator, delay mechanism (if needed), igniter, and incendiary material.

f. Initiator. The source that provides the first fire in an incendiary system. A match is an initiator. The initiator is so sensitive that it can be set off with little energy.

g. Spontaneous Combustion. The outbreak of fire in combustible material that occurs without an application of direct spark or flame. The fire is the result of heat produced by the chemical action of certain oils.

h. Thermite. An incendiary mixture of iron oxide flakes and aluminum powder that reacts chemically when initiated to form molten iron. Thermite can be used to burn holes in steel or to weld steel parts together.

0003. TOOLS AND TECHNIQUES

a. The equipment needed for the manufacture of incendiaries consists of simple items. They are all readily available. Required are bottles, jars, pots, and spoons. There should be no difficulty in obtaining any of them. All of the necessary equipment is described in each paragraph dealing with a particular incendiary component.

b. It is important that the operator follow the directions given in this manual *exactly* as written. They have been worked out carefully to give the desired results with the minimum chance of mishap. Don't experiment with different procedures or quantities.

c. By its very nature, the manufacture of incendiaries is dangerous. It is the function of incendiaries to burn with an intense flame under the right conditions. Care must be taken that no fires result during the making or placing of the devices. There are also other dangers in addition to the fire hazard. The chemicals used as ingredients may burn the skin, give off poisonous fumes, or be easily flammable. They must not be eaten.

d. When handled with care and proper precautions, incendiaries are fairly safe to make and use. Detailed precautions and instructions are given in each paragraph where they apply. General safety precautions follow:

Preventing a Fire Hazard

1. Fire prevention is much more important than fire fighting. Prevent fires from starting.

2. Keep flammable liquids away from open flames.

3. Good housekeeping is the fire prevention. Keep work areas neat and orderly. Clean away all equipment and material not needed at the moment. Clean up spills as soon as possible.

4. Store incendiaries in closed containers away from heat. Do not store material any longer than necessary.

5. In the event of fire, remove the incendiaries from the danger area if this can be done quickly and safely. Use large quantities of water to fight fires.

6. Horse play is dangerous and absolutely intolerable.

Avoiding Chemical Hazards

1. Wear rubber gloves, apron, and glasses when handling concentrated chemicals if at all possible.

2. Avoid inhaling fumes. Perform reactions in a well ventilated area or out of doors because the boiling is often violent and large amounts of fumes are given off that are poisonous if breathed too much.

3. Avoid acid contact with the skin. If chemicals are spilled on a person, wash immediately in running water for several minutes. If they splash in the eyes, wash the open eye in running water for at least 15 minutes.

4. Clean up any acid that is spilled on floor or bench by flushing with large amounts of water. Acid spilled on wood can cause a fire.

5. Always pour concentrated acids into water. Never pour water into concentrated acids because a violent reaction will occur.

CHAPTER 2
INITIATORS

0101. FUSE CORD

a. Description.
(1) This item consists of a continuous train of explosive or fastburning material enclosed in a flexible waterproof cord or cable. It is used for setting off an explosive or a combustible mixture of powders by action of the fuse flame on the material to be ignited. Fuse cord can be initiated by a match flame, using a specific procedure, or with a standard U.S. Army fuse lighter. Fuse cord burns at a uniform rate allowing the user to be away from the immediate scene when the incendiary actually functions.
(2) Fuse cord does not directly ignite any incendiaries listed in chapter 4 but is a primary initiator for all igniters listed in chapter 3 except: Potassium Permanganate—Glycer in (0206), Powdered Aluminum—Sulfur Pellets (0207), White Phosphorus (0209), and Subigniter For Thermite (0211).

b. Material and Equipment. Two Standard U.S. Army fuse cords are available:

8

(1) *Blasting time fuse.*

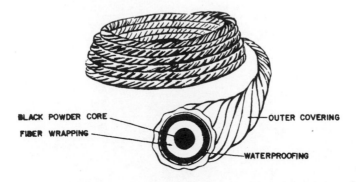

BLACK POWDER CORE

FIBER WRAPPING

OUTER COVERING

WATERPROOFING

This consists of black powder tightly wrapped with several layers of fabric and waterproofing materials. It might be any color, orange being the most common. The diameter of this fuse cord is 0.2 inch (a little larger than $\frac{3}{16}$ inch). This fuse burns inside the wrapping at a rate of approximately 40 seconds per foot. It must be tested before use to verify the burning rate.

(2) *Safety fuse M700.*

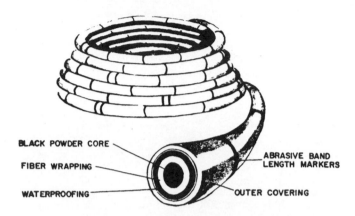

BLACK POWDER CORE

FIBER WRAPPING

WATERPROOFING

ABRASIVE BAND LENGTH MARKERS

OUTER COVERING

This fuse is similar to Blasting Time Fuse and may be used interchangeably with it. The fuse is a dark green cord 0.2 inch in diameter with a plastic cover, either smooth or with single painted abrasive bands around the outside at 1 foot or 18 inch intervals and double painted abrasive bands at 5 foot or 90 inch intervals depending on the time of manufacture. These bands are provided to make measuring easy. They are abrasive so that they can be felt in the dark. The fuse burns inside the wrapping at a rate of approximately 40 seconds per foot. It must be tested before use to verify the burning rate.

Note. A commercial item can be substituted for either of the above U.S. Army issue items. The commercial fuse is 0.1 inch (about ⅓₂ inch) in diameter and is coated only with waterproofing lacquer. This fuse can be easily ignited by holding the free end in a match flame because the outside covering if flammable.

c. Preparation. None.

d. Application.

  (1) *General.*

   (*a*) Cut and discard a 6-inch length from the free end of the fuse roll. Do this to be sure that there is no chance of misfire from a damp powder train because of absorption of moisture from the open air. Then cut off a measured length of fuze to check the burning rate. Check the burning rate before actual use.

   (*b*) Cut the fuse long enough to allow a reasonable time delay in initiation of the incendiary system. The cut should be made squarely across the fuse.

   (*c*) Prepare the fuse for ignition by splitting the fuse at one end to a depth of about one inch. Place the head of an unlighted match in the powder train.

   (*d*) Insert the other end of the fuse into a quantity of an igniter mixture so that the fuse end terminates near the center of the mixture. Be sure the fuse cord is anchored in the igniter mixture and cannot pull away. In the case of a solid igniter material such as Fire Fudge (0202), the fuse is split to about one-half inch at the end opposite the end containing the match in the powder train. This split fuse end is wedged over a sharp edge of the solid igniter material. Be sure the black powder in the fuse firmly contacts the solid igniter. If necessary, the fuse cord can be held firmly to the solid igniter with light tape such as transparent adhesive tape.

(e) The fuse is initiated by lighting the match head inserted in the split end of the fuse with a burning match as shown below.

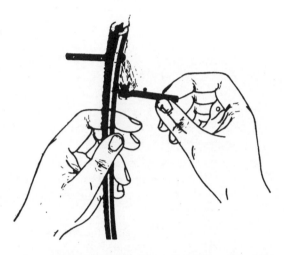

(f) Two standard fuse lighters, the M2 and M60, are available in demolition kits for positive lighting of Blasting Time Fuse and Safety Fuse M700 under all weather conditions—even under water if it is properly waterproofed. The devices are manually operated. A pull on the striker retaining pin causes the striker to hit the percussion primer, thus igniting the fuse. *These devices are not recommended where silence is required because a report is heard when the primer is fired.*

(2) *M2 fuse lighter.*

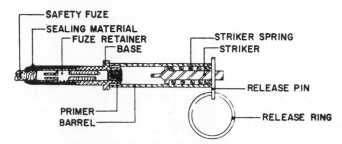

SAFETY FUZE
SEALING MATERIAL
FUZE RETAINER
BASE
STRIKER SPRING
STRIKER
RELEASE PIN
PRIMER
BARREL
RELEASE RING

The attachment and operation of the M2 Fuse Lighter are as follows:

(*a*) Slide the pronged fuse retainer over the end of the fuse and firmly seat it.

(*b*) Waterproof the joint between the fuse and the lighter, if necessary, by applying a sealing compound (putty or mastic).

(*c*) In firing, hold the barrel in one hand and pull on the release pin with the other hand.

(3) *M60 fuse lighter.*

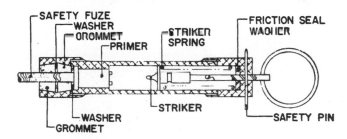

SAFETY FUZE
WASHER
GROMMET
PRIMER
STRIKER
SPRING
FRICTION SEAL
WASHER
STRIKER
WASHER
GROMMET
SAFETY PIN

The attachment and operation of the M60 Fuse Lighter are as follows:

(*a*) Unscrew the fuse holder cap two or three turns.

(*b*) Press the shipping plug into the lighter to release the split grommet, and rotate the plug as it is removed.

(*c*) Insert end of fuse in place of the plug until it rests against the primer.

(*d*) Tighten the fuse holder cap sufficiently to hold the fuse tightly in place and thus waterproof the joint.

(*e*) To fire, remove the safety pin, hold the barrel in one hand, and pull on the pull ring with the other hand.

›102. IMPROVISED STRING FUSE

a. Description.

IGNITER   STRING FUSE

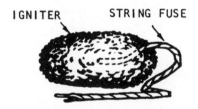

(1) This item consists of string, twine, or shoelaces that have been treated with either a mixture of potassium nitrate and granulated sugar or potassium chlorate and granulated sugar.

(2) Improvised string fuse does not directly ignite any incendiaries listed in chapter 4 but is a primary initiator for all igniters listed in chapter 3 except: Potassium Permanganate —Glycerin (0206), Powdered Aluminum—

Sulfur Pellets (0207), White Phosphorus (0209), and Subigniter For Thermite (0211).

(3) Depending upon the length of the fuse, the user can be away from the immediate scene when an incendiary system is initiated.

b. *Material and Equipment.*

String, twine or shoelaces made of cotton or linen.

Potassium nitrate or potassium chlorate.

Granulated sugar.

Small cooking pot.

Spoon.

Heat source such as stove or hot plate.

Soap.

c. *Preparation.*

(1) Wash string or shoelaces in hot soapy water; rinse in fresh water.

(2) Dissolve one part potassium nitrate or potassium chlorate and one part granulated sugar in two parts hot water.

(3) Soak string or shoelaces in the hot solution for at least five minutes.

(4) Remove the string from hot solution and twist or braid three strands of string together.

(5) Hang the fuse up to dry.

(6) Check actual burning rate of the fuse by measuring the time it takes for a known length to burn.

d. *Application.*

(1) This fuse does not have a waterproof coating and it must be tested by burning a measured length before actual use.

(2) Cut the fuse long enough to allow a reasonable time delay in initiation of the incendiary system.

(3) Insert one end of the fuse in a quantity of an igniter mixture so that the fuse end terminates near the center of the mixture. Be sure the fuse cord is anchored in the igniter mixture and cannot pull away. In the case of a solid igniter material such as Fire Fudge (0202), the improvised string fuse is securely wrapped around a piece of solid igniter material.

(4) The fuse is initiated by lighting the free end of the fuse with a match.

(5) This fuse does not burn when it is wet. Its use is not recommended where there is the possibility of the fuse getting wet.

0103. CONCENTRATED SULFURIC ACID (OIL OF VITRIOL)

a. Description.

(1) This material is a heavy, corrosive, oily, and colorless liquid. Storage is recommended in a glass container with a glass lid or stopper. Commercially available sulfuric acid is approximately 93 percent concentration with a specific gravity of 1.835. This is commonly referred to as concentrated sulfuric acid.

(2) Concentrated sulfuric acid chars wood, cotton, and vegetable fibers, usually without causing fire. The addition of water to concentrated sulfuric acid develops much heat which may be sufficient to cause a fire or an explosion. This depends upon the quantity of acid, quantity of water, and rate of addition of water.

Caution: **Always add concentrated sulfuric acid to water. Never add water to a concentrated acid.**

(3) Certain igniter materials can be reliably brought to flaming by the addition of concentrated sulfuric acid. This is brought about by the chemical reaction between the sulfuric acid and the igniter materials. The following igniters are initiated by concentrated sulfuric acid: Sugar-Chlorate (0201), Fire Fudge (0202), Sugar—Sodium Peroxide (0203), Aluminum Powder—Sodium Peroxide (0204), Match Head (0205), and Silver Nitrate—Magnesium Powder (0208).

(4) The most important use for concentrated sulfuric acid as an initiator is in conjunction with delay mechanisms. The acid is held away from the igniter for a period of time by making use of the corrosive action of the acid to work its way through a barrier. If the delay mechanism is placed in a cold environment, the concentrated acid will remain fluid at extremely low temperatures. The following delay mechanisms are recommended for use with concentrated sulfuric acid: Gelatin Capsule (0402), Rubber Diaphragm (0403), Paper Diaphragm (0404), Tipping Delay—Filled tube (0408), Tipping Delay— Balancing Stick (0410), and Stretched Rubber Band (0411).

b. Material and Equipment. Concentrated sulfuric acid.

c. Preparation. None—If only battery-grade sulfuric acid is available (specific gravity 1.200), it must be concentrated before use to a specific gravity of 1.835. This is done by heating it in an enameled, heat-resistant glass or porcelain pot until dense, white fumes appear. Heat only in a well ventilated area. When dense, white fumes start to appear, remove the heat and allow acid to cool. Store the concentrated acid in a glass container.

    d. Application.

        (1) *General.* Commercial sulfuric acid is available in 13 gallon carboys. Smaller quantities of this acid are available in chemical laboratory reagent storage containers. It is recommended that a small quantity of acid, about one pint, be secured and stored in a glass container until it is used.

        (2) *Use with delay mechanisms.*

            (a) Construction of specific delay mechanisms is described in chapter 5. Within the delay mechanism, there is a container filled with acid. The acid corrodes this container, is absorbed by the container material or is spilled from the container until it comes in contact with the igniter mixture.

            (b) Carefully fill the container in the delay mechanism with concentrated sulfuric acid. This can be accomplished easily with a small glass funnel. A medicine dropper is used when the delay mechanism container is small.

Caution: **Concentrated sulfuric acid must be handled carefully because it is very corrosive. If it is splashed on clothing, skin or eyes, the affected area must be immediately flushed with water. This may not be always practical. It is recommended that eye protection be worn by the user when pouring concentrated sulfuric acid. Many types are** available for this purpose. Rubber gloves can be worn to protect the hands. A small bottle of water can be carried to flush small areas of skin or clothing which may be contaminated with the acid.

(3) *Manual application.*

    (*a*) Manual application of concentrated sulfuric acid for direct initiation of an igniter is not recommended when fuse cord is available. It is possible to employ this acid for direct initiation by quickly adding three or four drops to the igniter material. This can be accomplished with a medicine dropper. Keep hands and clothing clear of the igniter; ignition may take place almost instantly with addition of acid.

Caution: **Do not allow material such as sugar, wood, cotton or woolen fibers to fall into the** *boiling acid.* **A violent reaction could occur with splattering of acid.**

    (*b*) Since sulfuric acid has a unique freezing point related to acid concentration, the information shown below is useful when this acid is used with delay mechanisms in low temperature surroundings. Be sure of acid concentration by checking with a hydrometer.

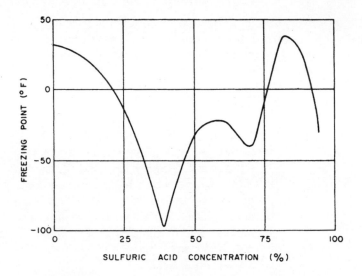

SULFURIC   ACID   CONCENTRATION   (%)

Sulfuric acid concentration (%)	Specific gravity	Freezing point (° F.)
0	1.000	+32
10	1.074	+23
20	1.151	+5
30	1.229	−39
39	1.295	−97
40	1.306	−91
50	1.408	−31
60	1.510	−22
70	1.611	−40
75	1.686	−7
77	1.706	+12
80	1.726	+27
81	1.747	+39
89	1.818	+24
90	1.824	+13
92	1.830	−1
93	1.835	−29

0104. WATER

a. *Description.*

(1) Water causes spontaneous initiation of certain igniter mixtures. This is caused by a chemical reaction of the igniter materials in the presence of water. The following igniters are initiated by water: Sugar—Sodium Peroxide (0203), Aluminum Powder—Sodium Peroxide (0204), and Silver Nitrate—Magnesium Powder (0208).

(2) The most important use for water as an initiator is in conjunction with delay mechanisms. Since only a few igniter mixtures are initiated by water and *it cannot be used at freezing temperatures,* its use is limited. When tactics so dictate, water can be reliably used with the following delay mechanisms: Gelatin Capsule (0402), Overflow (0407), Tipping Delay—Filled Tube (0408), Balancing Stick (0410), and Stretched Rubber Band (0411).

Note. Sulfuric acid of any concentration can be substituted for water in the initiation of water activated igniters. Water *cannot* be substituted for concentrated sulfuric acid.

b. *Material and Equipment.* Water.

c. *Preparation.* None.

d. *Application.*

(1) *Use with delay mechanisms.* Construction of specific delay mechanisms is presented in chapter 5. Within the delay mechanism, there is a container filled with water. The water dissolves the container or is spilled from the container and comes in contact with igniter mixture, initiating the fire train.

(2) *Manual application.* Fuse cord, when available, is recommended in preference to water as an initiator. Water is used for direct ignition of a specific igniter by adding drops as with a medicine dropper. Keep hands and clothing clear of the igniter; ignition may take place almost instantaneously with addition of water.

CHAPTER 3
IGNITERS

0201. SUGAR-CHLORATE

a. Description.

(1) This item consists of a mixture of granulated sugar and potassium chlorate or sodium chlorate. It can be used to ignite all the incendiaries listed in chapter 4 except Thermite (0307). It may be used directly as an incendiary on readily flammable material such as rags, dry paper, dry hay, or in the combustible vapor above liquid fuels.

(2) The igniter can be initiated by Fuse Cord (0101), Improvised String Fuse (0102), or Concentrated Sulfuric Acid (0103).

(3) This simple sugar-chlorate mixture closely resembles granulated sugar and should not ordinarily arouse suspicion. It is an excellent igniter.

Caution: **This mixture is poisonous and must not be eaten.**

b. Material and Equipment.

Granulated sugar (do *not* use powdered or confectioners sugar.)

Potassium chlorate or sodium chlorate (no coarser than granulated sugar).

Spoon (preferably nonmetallic).

Container with tight-fitting lid.

Rolling pin or round stick.

c. Preparation.

    (1) Using a clean, dry spoon, place granulated sugar in the container to one-quarter container volume. Wipe the spoon with a clean cloth.

    (2) If the potassium or sodium chlorate is lumpy, remove all lumps by crushing with a rolling pin. Using the spoon, add an equal quantity of chlorate to the container.

    Caution: **If this mixture is carelessly handled with excessive bumping and scraping, It could be a fire hazard to the user. As a precaution, remove any mixture adhering to the lip or edge of the jar before tightening the lid.**

    (3) Tighten the lid of the jar, turn the jar on its side and slowly roll until the two powders are completely mixed. The mixture is now ready for use. It may be stored for months in a tightly sealed container.

d. Application.

    (1) Carefully pour or spoon the mixture, in a single pile, on the incendiary. Prepare the mixture for ignition with Fuse Cord (0101) or Improvised String Fuse (0102) in the normal manner. The fuse cord should terminate near the center of the igniter mixture. Concentrated Sulfuric Acid (0103) can be used as an initiator, but is generally less convenient. Ignition takes place almost immediately on contact with the acid. Acid is recommended for use with specific delay mechanisms found in chapter 5.

    (2) If only battery-grade sulfuric acid is available, it must be concentrated before use to a

specific gravity of 1.835 by heating it in an enameled, heat-resistant glass or porcelain pot until dense, white fumes start to appear. See paragraph 0103 for details.

(3) When used to ignite flammable liquids, wrap a quantity of the mixture in a nonabsorbent material and suspend it inside the container near the open top. The container must remain open for easy ignition and combustion of the flammable liquid.

(4) To minimize the hazard of premature ignition of flammable liquid vapors, allow at least two feet of fuse length to extend from the top edge of an open container of flammable liquid before lighting the fuse.

0202. FIRE FUDGE

a. *Description.*

(1) This item consists of a mixture of sugar and potassium chlorate in a hot water solution which solidifies when cooled to room temperature. It can be used to ignite all the incendiaries listed in chapter 4 except Thermite (0307). It may be used directly as an incendiary on readily flammable material, such as rags, dry paper, dry hay, or in the combustible vapor above liquid fuels.

(2) The igniter can be initiated by Fuse Cord (0101), Improvised String Fuse (0102), or Concentrated Sulfuric Acid (0103).

(3) Fire fudge resembles a white sugar fudge having a smooth, hard surface. The advantage of this igniter material over Sugar-Chlorate (0201), is its moldability. The

procedure for preparation must be followed closely to obtain a smooth, uniform material with a hard surface.

Caution: **This material is poisonous and must not be eaten.**

b. *Material and Equipment.*

Granulated sugar (do *not* use powdered or confectioners sugar).

Potassium chlorate (no coarser than granulated sugar).

Metallic, glass or enameled pan.

Measuring container (size of this container determines quantity of finished product).

Spoon (preferably nonmetallic).

Thermometer (to read in the range 200° F. to 250° F.)

Heat source.

c. *Preparation.*

(1) Clean the pan by boiling some clean water in it for about five minutes. Discard the water, pour one measureful of clean water into the pan and warm it. Dry the measuring container and add one measureful of sugar. Stir the liquid until the sugar dissolves.

(2) Boil the solution until a fairly thick syrup is obtained.

(3) Remove the pan from the source of heat to a distance of at least six feet and shut off heat. Rapidly add two measurefuls of potassium chlorate. Stir gently for a minute to mix the syrup and powder, then pour or spoon the mixture into appropriate molds. If the mold is paper, it can usually be peeled off when the fire fudge cools and hardens. Pieces of card-

board or paper adhering to the igniter will not impair its use. Pyrex glass or ceramic molds can be used when a clear, smooth surface if desired. It is recommended that section thickness of molded fire fudge be at least one-half inch. If desired, molded fire fudge can be safely broken with the fingers.

(4) This material is moderately hard immediately after cooling. It will become harder after 24 hours. When kept in a tightly sealed container, it will retain its effectiveness for months.

Caution: **If this igniter material is carelessly handled with excessive bumping -or scraping, it could be a fire hazard to the user.**

d. *Application.*

(1) Place a piece of fire fudge on top of the incendiary. Minimum size should be about one inch square and one-half inch thick Prepare the fire fudge for ignition with Fuse Cord (0101) or Improvised String Fuse (0102) in the normal manner. Concentrated Sulfuric Acid (0103) can be used as an initiator but is generally less convenient. Acid is recommended for use with specific delay mechanisms found in chapter 5.

(2) If only battery-grade sulfuric acid is available it must be concentrated before use to a specific gravity of 1.835 by heating it in an enameled, heat resistant glass or porcelain pot until dense, white fumes start to appear. See paragraph 0103 for details.

(3) When used to ignite flammable liquids, wrap a quantity of the igniter mixture in a non-absorbent material and suspend it inside the container near the open top. The container must remain open for easy ignition and combustion of the flammable liquid.

(4) To minimize the hazard of premature ignition of flammable liquid vapors, allow at least two feet of fuse length to extend from the top edge of an open container of flammable liquid before lighting the fuse.

0203. SUGAR—SODIUM PEROXIDE

a. *Description.*

(1) This item consists of a mixture of sodium peroxide and granulated sugar. It can be used to ignite all the incendiaries listed in chapter 4 except Thermite (0307). It may be used directly as an incendiary on readily flammable material such as rags, dry paper dry hay, or in the combustible vapor above liquid fuels.

(2) The igniter can be initiated by Fuse Cord (0101), Improvised String Fuse (0102), Concentrated Sulfuric Acid (0103), or Water (0104).

Caution: **This mixture is unstable and can ignite at high humidity or when wet slightly by drops of water, perspiration, etc.**

b. *Material and Equipment.*

Granulated sugar (do *not* use powdered or confectioners sugar).

Sodium peroxide (no coarser than granulated sugar).

Spoon.
Container with tight fitting lid for mixing and
storage.

c. *Preparation.*

(1) Using a clean, dry spoon, place granulated
sugar in the container to one-quarter container
volume.

(2) Wipe the spoon with a clean, dry cloth, and
add an equal amount of sodium peroxide to
the dry mixing container. Tighten the lid on
the sodium peroxide container, and remove it
at least six feet from the working area.

(3) Tighten the lid on the mixing container. Turn
the container on its side and slowly roll until
the two powders are completely mixed. The
mixture is now ready for use.

(4) A good practice is to keep the granulated
sugar and sodium peroxide in separate air-
tight containers and mix just before use.

Caution: **Do not store this mixture longer
than three days because decomposition may
occur and cause spontaneous combustion.
Be sure that the storage container is air-tight.**

d. *Application.*

(1) Carefully pour or spoon the mixture, in a
single pile, on the incendiary. Prepare the
mixture for ignition with Fuse Cord (0101)
or Improvised String Fuse (0102) in the
normal manner. The fuse cord should
terminate near the center of the igniter
mixture. Concentrated Sulfuric Acid (0103)
and Water (0104) can be used as initiators, but
are generally less convenient. Ignition takes
place almost immediately on contact with the

acid or water. These liquid initiators are convenient for use with specific delay mechanisms found in chapter 5.

(2) When used to ignite flammable liquids, wrap a quantity of the mixture in a non-absorbent material and suspend it inside the container near the open top. The container must remain open for easy ignition and combustion of the flammable liquid.

(3) To minimize the hazard of premature ignition of flammable liquid vapors, allow at least two feet of fuse length to extend from the top of an open container of flammable liquid before lighting the fuse.

0204. ALUMINUM POWDER—SODIUM PEROXIDE

a. Description.

(1) This item consists of a mixture of sodium peroxide and powdered aluminum. It can be used to ignite all the incendiaries listed in chapter 4 except Thermite (0307). It may be used directly as an incendiary on readily flammable material, such as rags, dry paper, dry hay or in the combustible vapor above liquid fuels.

(2) The igniter can be initiated by Fuse Cord (0101), Improvised String Fuse (0102), Concentrated Sulfuric Acid (0103), or water (0104).

Caution: **This mixture is unstable and can ignite at high humidity or when wet slightly by drops of water, perspiration, etc.**

b. Material and Equipment.

Powdered aluminum (no coarser than granulated sugar).

Sodium peroxide no coarser than granulated sugar).

Spoon.

Container with tight fitting lid for mixing and storage.

c. Preparation.

(1) Using a clean, dry spoon, place powdered aluminum in the container to one-quarter container volume.

(2) Wipe the spoon with a clean, dry cloth, and add an equal amount of sodium peroxide to the dry mixing container. Tighten the lid on the sodium peroxide container, and remove it at least six feet from the working area.

(3) Tighten the lid of the mixing container. Turn the container on its side and slowly roll until the two powders are completely mixed. The mixture is now ready to use.

(4) A good practice is to keep the powdered aluminum and sodium peroxide in separate containers and mix just before use.

Caution: Do not store this mixture longer than three days because decomposition may occur and cause spontaneous combustion. Be sure that the storage container is air-tight.

d. Application.

(1) Carefully pour or spoon the mixture, in a single pile, on the incendiary. Prepare the mixture for ignition with Fuse Cord (0101) or Improvised String Fuse (0102) in the normal manner. The fuse cord should terminate

near the center of the igniter mixture. Concentrated Sulfuric Acid (0103) and Water (0104) can be used as initiators, but are generally less convenient. Ignition takes place almost immediately on contact with the acid or water. These liquid initiators are convenient for use with specific delay mechanisms found in (chapter 5.)

(2) When used to ignite flammable liquids, wrap a quantity of the mixture in a nonabsorbent material and suspend it inside the container near the open top. The container must remain open for easy ignition and combustion of the flammable liquid.

(3) To minimize the hazard of premature ignition of flammable liquid vapors, allow at least two feet of fuse length to extend from the top edge of an open container of flammable liquid before lighting the fuse.

0205. MATCH HEAD

a. Description.

(1) This item consists of a quantity of match heads, prepared by breaking the heads off their match sticks and grouping the match heads together to form the desired quantity of igniter. Any kind of friction match will do. It can be used to ignite the following incendiaries listed in chapter 4: Napalm (0301), Gelled Gasoline (exotic thickeners) (0302), Gelled Gasoline (improvised thickeners) (0303), Paraffin-Sawdust (0304), and Flammable Liquids (0308). It may be used directly

as an incendiary on readily flammable material such as rags, dry paper, dry hay or in the combustible vapor above liquid fuels.

(2) The igniter can be initiated by a match flame, Fuse Cord (0101), Improvised String Fuse (0102), or Concentrated Sulfuric Acid (0103).

b. *Material and Equipment.*

Razor blade or knife.

Container with tight-fitting lid.

Matches, friction.

c. *Preparation.*

(1) Using a knife or razor blade, cut off the match heads.

(2) Prepare the desired quantity of igniter and store it in an airtight container until ready for use.

d. *Application.*

(1) Pour or spoon the match heads, in a single pile, on the incendiary. Prepare the match heads for ignition with Fuse Cord (0101) or Improvised String Fuse (0102) in the normal manner. The fuse cord should terminate near the center of the match head pile. Concentrated Sulfuric Acid (0103) or a match flame can also be used as an initiator. Ignition takes place almost immediately on contact with the acid or the match flame. Acid is recommended for use with specific delay mechanisms found in chapter 5.

(2) If only battery-grade sulfuric acid is available, it must be concentrated before use to a specific gravity of 1.835 by heating it in an enameled, heat-resistant glass or porcelain

pot until dense, white fumes start to appear. See paragraph 0103 for details.

(3) When used to ignite flammable liquids, wrap a quantity of the match heads in a non-absorbent material and suspend it inside the container near the open top. The container must remain open for easy ignition and combustion of the flammable liquid.

(4) To minimize the hazard of premature ignition of flammable liquid vapors, allow at least two feet of fuse length to extend from the top edge of an open container of flammable liquid before lighting the fuse.

0206. POTASSIUM PERMANGANATE—GLYCERIN

a. *Description.*

(1) This item consists of a small pile of potassium permanganate crystals which are ignited by the chemical action of glycerin on the crystals. It can be used to ignite all the incendiaries listed in chapter 4 except Thermite (0307). It may be used directly as an incendiary on readily flammable material, such as rags, dry paper, dry hay, or in the combustible vapor above liquid fuels.

(2) Ignition is accomplished by causing a few drops of glycerin to contact the potassium permanganate crystals. A hotter flame is produced when powdered magnesium or powdered aluminum is mixed with the the potassium permanganate crystals.

(3) Ignition time, after addition of the glycerin, increases as temperature decreases. This igniter is not reliable below 50° F.

b. *Material and Equipment.*

Potassium permanganate crystals (no coarser than granulated sugar).

Glycerin.

One small container with tight-fitting lid for the glycerin.

One larger container with tight-fitting lid for the potassium permanganate crystals.

Powdered magnesium or powdered aluminum (no coarser than granulated sugar).

Preparation.

(1) Put some glycerin in the small container and cap tightly.

(2) Fill the larger container with potassium permanganate crystals and cap tightly.

(3) If powdered magnesium or powdered aluminum is available, mix 85 parts potassium permanganate crystals and 15 parts powdered magnesium or powdered aluminum and store this mixture in the large bottle.

(4) Keep these containers tightly sealed and the material in the containers will remain effective for a long period of time.

d. *Application.* Pour out a quantity of the potassium permanganate crystals (with or without powdered aluminum or powdered magnesium), in a single pile on the incendiary. Manual ignition is accomplished by causing a few drops of glycerin from a medicine dropper to come in contact with the potassium permanganate crystals. Keep hands and clothing clear of the igniter; ignition may take place almost instantly with addition of the glycerin. This igniter is convenient for use with specific delay mechanisms found in chapter 5.

0207. POWDERED ALUMINUM—SULFUR PELLETS

a. Description.

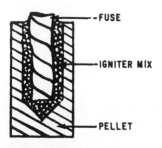

(1) This igniter consists of finely powdered aluminum, sulfur and starch which have been thoroughly mixed and shaped into hardened cylindrical pellets. It can be used to ignite all the incendiaries listed in chapter 4. It is an excellent igniter for Thermite (0307). It may be used directly as an incendiary on readily flammable material such as rags, dry paper, dry hay, or in the combustible vapor above liquid fuels.

(2) The igniter can be initiated by Fuse Cord (0101) or Improvised String Fuse (0102). A hole is made in one pellet to receive a fuse and a small quantity of another more easily started igniter mixture. A number of unmodified pellets are attached to the first pellet to increase the quantity of heat after combustion occurs.

b. Material and Equipment.

Finely powdered aluminum (no coarser than cake flour).

TAGO 7189-C

Finely powdered sulfur (no coarser than cake flour).

Finely powdered starch (no coarser than cake flour).

Water.

Cylindrical tube about 4 inches long and $\frac{3}{4}$ inch inside diameter made of metal, wood, glass or plastic.

Rod which fits into the above tube.

Rod about $\frac{3}{8}$ inch in diameter (should be about one-half the inside diameter of the 4-inch long tube).

Mixing bowl.

Tablespoon.

Teaspoon.

Stove or hot plate.

Knife.

Measuring container.

c. *Preparation.*

(1) Place six tablespoons of aluminum powder in a mixing bowl then add 15 tablespoons of powdered sulfur.

(2) Mix the two powders gently with the spoon for a few minutes until no unmixed particles of sulfur are visible.

(3) In a separate pot add two teaspoons of laundry starch to about 6 ounces of water and boil gently for a few minutes. Stir until the starch is dissolved and allow the solution to cool to room temperature.

(4) When cool, take about one-half of the starch solution and add it to the mixture of aluminum and sulfur powder.

(5) Mix with a spoon until the whole mass is a smooth, evenly mixed, putty-like paste.

(6) Fill the cylindrical tube with this paste, place one end of this tube on a hard surface and tamp the paste with the $\frac{3}{8}$ inch diameter rod to squeeze out the air bubbles and consolidate the paste.

(7) Push the paste out of the tube with the larger rod, which just fits the tube, so that it forms a cylinder, then cut the damp cylinder into $1\frac{1}{2}$ inch lengths using the knife.

(8) Dry these pieces at 90° F. for at least 24 hours before using. The drying time can be reduced by using a drying oven at a maximum temperature of 150° F.

(9) Form a hole at least $\frac{1}{2}$ inch in diameter approximately half-way into one end of an igniter pellet.

(10) Put one of the following igniters into the cavity to roughly one-half its depth:
Sugar-Chlorate (0201)
Sugar—Sodium Peroxide (0203)
Aluminum Powder—Sodium Peroxide (0204)
Silver Nitrate—Magnesium Powder (0208)

(11) Insert a length of fuse into the hole so that it makes contact with the igniter mix. Fill the remainder of the hole with igniter mix and tamp down to hold the fuse firmly.

(12) Tape the fuse cord in place to prevent it from working loose and falling out.

(13) Tape two or more pellets without holes to the one with the fuse.

(14) Store all the pellets in a dry, closed container until required for use.

d. Application.

(1) For ignition of thermite, a cluster of at least three pellets should be used. Bury the cluster of igniter pellets just below the surface of the thermite, with the fuse extending for ignition by a match flame. Large quantities of thermite may require a cluster of more than three pellets for satisfactory ignition.

(2) For use as an igniter of a solid incendiary, place a cluster of pellets on top of the incendiary.

(3) When used to ignite flammable liquids, wrap a cluster of igniter pellets in a nonabsorbent material and suspend it inside the container near the open top. The container must remain open for easy ignition and combustion of the flammable liquid.

(4) To minimize the hazard of premature ignition of flammable liquid vapors, allow at least two feet of fuse length to extend from the top edge of an open container of flammable liquid before lighting the fuse.

0208. SILVER NITRATE—MAGNESIUM POWDER

a. Description.

(1) This item consists of a mixture of silver nitrate crystals and magnesium powder. It can be used to ignite all the incendiaries listed in chapter 4 except Thermite (0307). It may be used directly as an incendiary on readily flammable material such as rags, dry paper, dry hay, or in the combustible vapor above liquid fuels.

(2) The igniter can be initiated by Fuse Cord (0101), Improvised String Fuse (0102), Concentrated Sulfuric Acid (0103), or Water (0104).

Caution: **This mixture is unstable and may ignite at high humidity or when wet slightly by drops of water, perspiration, etc.**

b. *Material and Equipment.*

Silver nitrate crystals (no coarser than granulated sugar).

Magnesium powder or filings (no coarser than granulated sugar).

Spoon.

Container with tight-fitting lid.

c. *Preparation.*

(1) Using a clean, dry spoon, place magnesium powder or filings into the dry mixing container to one-quarter container volume. If magnesium filings are used, they should be free of grease.

(2) Wipe the spoon with a clean, dry cloth, then add an equal quantity of silver nitrate crystals to the dry mixing container. Tighten the lid on the silver nitrate container, and remove it at least six feet from the working area.

(3) Tightly close the lid on the mixing container. Turn the container on its side and slowly roll until the two powders are completely mixed. The mixture is now ready for use.

(4) A good practice is to keep the silver nitrate crystals and the magnesium powder or filings in separate air-tight containers and mix just before use.

Caution: This mixture should be kept out of direct sunlight to avoid decomposition of the silver nitrate which could render this igniter mixture ineffective.

d. *Application.*

(1) Carefully pour or spoon the mixture, in a single pile, on the incendiary. Prepare the mixture for ignition with either Fuse Cord (0101) or Improvised String Fuse (0102) in the normal manner. The fuse cord should terminate near the center of the igniter mixture. Concentrated Sulfuric Acid (0103) and Water (0104) can be used as initiators but are generally less convenient. Ignition takes place almost immediately on contact with the acid or water. These liquid initiators are convenient for use with specific delay mechanisms found in chapter 5.

(2) When used to ignite flammable liquids, wrap a quantity of the mixture in a nonabsorbent material and suspend it inside the container near the open top. The container must remain open for easy ignition and combustion of the flammable liquid.

(3) To minimize the hazard of premature ignition of flammable liquid vapors, allow at least two feet of fuse length to extend from the top edge of an open container of flammable liquid before lighting the fuse.

0209. WHITE PHOSPHORUS

a. *Description.*

(1) This item consists of white phosphorus dissolved in carbon disulfide. It can be used to

ignite the following incendiaries listed in chapter 4: Napalm (0301), Gelled Gasoline (exotic thickeners) (0302), Gelled Gasoline (improvised thickeners) (0303), and Paraffin-Sawdust (0304). It may be used directly as an incendiary on readily flammable material such as rags, dry paper, dry hay, or in the combustible vapor above liquid fuels.

(2) Ignition is achieved when the volatile solvent, carbon disulfide, evaporates and the white phosphorus comes in contact with air.

Caution: **Never touch white phosphorus directly or allow any of its solutions to touch the skin. Painful burns which heal very slowly may result. White phosphorus sticks must** *always* **be stored completely under water. If any of the phosphorus solution is accidently spilled on the skin, immediately flush the affected area with water; then decontaminate the affected area by dabbing with copper sulfate solution.**

b. *Material and Equipment.*

White phosphorus sticks (sometimes called yellow phosphorus).

Carbon disulfide.

Copper sulfate solution.

Tweezers or tongs.

Two glass containers about 8-ounce capacity with lids or stoppers made of glass, earthenware, or metal. Do not use a rubber lid or stopper (carbon disulfide will attack rubber).

c. *Preparation.*

(1) Prepare some copper sulfate solution by adding one spoonful of copper sulfate crystals

to one of the glass containers. Fill the container with water, place the stopper in the open mouth of the bottle and shake until the crystals dissolve.

(2) Pour carbon disulfide into the other glass container to one-quarter container volume.

Caution: **Carbon disulfide fumes are poisonous. Always cap an open container of carbon disulfide as soon as possible. Work in a well ventilated area.**

(3) With a pair of tweezers remove some sticks of white phosphorus from their storage container. Totally submerge them immediately in the carbon disulfide to bring the level up to one-half full. Be sure that all the phosphorus left in the original container is completely submerged in water before putting the container away. Wash the tweezers immediately in the copper sulfate solution.

(4) Securely stopper the bottle containing the white phosphorus and carbon disulfide and allow to stand until the white phosphorus dissolves. This usually takes about eight hours. The time required to dissolve white phosphorus can be reduced by shaking the bottle. Be sure that the bottle top does not come off.

(5) Do not store in direct sunlight because the solution will become ineffective. This solution should never be stored more than three days.

Note. If carbon disulfide is not available, benzene (benzol) may be used to dissolve the phosphorus. It requires considerable shaking and overnight soaking to get an appreciable amount of phosphorus dissolved in benzene. *Do not* attempt to use red phosphorus for preparing this igniter because it does not behave like white phosphorus.

d. Application.

(1) To ignite readily flammable material, pour the white phosphorus solution directly onto the material; it will ignite when the solvent evaporates, exposing the white phosphorus to the air. Once the solution is poured, the empty bottle should be discarded immediately because any solution remaining on the bottle will ignite when the solvent evaporates. Do not cover the soaked flammable material because the carbon disulfide must evaporate for ignition to occur.

(2) The incendiaries mentioned under *Description* above can be initiated by first impregnating crumpled paper or absorbent paper towels with the white phosphorus solution and placing the impregnated paper on the material to be ignited.

(3) Delay times of the phosphorus solution may be varied by the addition of gasoline or toluene (toluol). Add a small quantity of either solvent to the original white phosphorus solution and test the solution each time until the desired delay time is achieved. Delay times of 20 to 30 minutes may be obtained in this manner.

(4) Check the delay time under conditions expected at the target. Air currents hasten the evaporation of the solvent and decrease delay time. A high ambient temperature will also decrease delay time whereas a low ambient

temperature will increase the delay time. This igniter is not reliable at or below freezing temperatures (32° F.)

(5) To make incendiary paper, soak strips of ordinary writing paper in the phosphorus-carbon disulfide for a few minutes. Remove the paper with a pair of tweezers or tongs and place in a vial filled with water. Be sure to wash off the tweezers immediately in copper sulfide solution. Cap the vial and store until ready to use. To use this incendiary paper, remove the strips of paper with a pair of tweezers, and place among the material to be ignited.

0210. MAGNESIUM POWDER—BARIUM PEROXIDE

a. *Description.*

(1) This item consists of a mixture of finely powdered magnesium and finely powdered barium peroxide. It can be used to ignite all the incendiaries listed in chapter 4 and is particularly suited for ignition of thermite. It may be used directly as an incendiary on readily flammable material such as rags, dry paper, dry hay, or in the combustible vapor above liquid fuels.

(2) The igniter can be initiated by Fuse Cord (0101) or Improvised String Fuse (0102).

b. *Material and Equipment.*

Magnesium powder (no coarser than table salt).
Barium peroxide (no coarser than table salt).
Spoon.
Container with tight-fitting lid.

c. Preparation.

(1) Using a clean, dry spoon, place powdered magnesium into the dry mixing container to one-quarter container volume.

(2) Wipe the spoon with a clean, dry cloth, then add powdered barium peroxide to the dry mixing container to three-quarters container volume. Tighten the lid on the barium peroxide container, and remove it at least six feet from the working area.

(3) Tightly close the lid on the mixing container. Turn the container on its side and slowly roll until the two powders are completely mixed. The mixture is now ready for use.

(4) A good practice is to keep the powdered magnesium and powdered barium peroxide in separate containers and mix just before use.

d. Application.

(1) Carefully pour or spoon the mixture, in a single pile, onto the incendiary. Prepare the mixture for ignition with Fuse Cord (0101) or Improvised String Fuse (0102) in the normal manner. The fuse cord should terminate near the center of the igniter mixture.

(2) In ignition of thermite, spread the igniter mixture to a depth of at least $\frac{1}{4}$ inch on the top surface of the thermite which is held in an assembly described under *Application* of Thermite incendiary (0307). The fuse cord will initiate the thermite igniter which will, in turn, ignite the thermite.

(3) When used to ignite flammable liquids, wrap a quantity of the mixture in a nonabsorbent material and suspend it inside the container

near the open top. The container must remain open for easy ignition and combustion of the flammable liquid.

(4) To minimize the hazard of premature ignition of flammable liquid vapors, allow at least two feet of fuse length to extend from the top edge of an open container of flammable liquid before lighting the fuse.

0211. SUBIGNITER FOR THERMITE

a. *Description.*

(1) This item consists of a mixture of a metal powder and an oxidizing agent. Two metal powder alternates and four oxidizing agent alternates are specified. In the combustion process, the metal powder is oxidized, resulting in the liberation of a large quantity of heat.

(2) This subigniter is a substitute for Magnesium Powder–Barium Peroxide Igniter (0210), and should be used only if that Igniter is not available. The disadvantage of this subigniter is that it cannot be directly initiated by fuse cord. To use this subigniter for initiating thermite, it is necessary to use another igniter mixture to initiate the subigniter, preferably Sugar-Chlorate (0201). The fuse cord will initiate the sugar-chlorate, which will, in turn, ignite the subigniter and, thereby, initiate the thermite.

(3) This subigniter can be directly initiated by all the igniters listed in chapter 3 except White Phosphorus (0209).

b. Material and Equipment.

Either aluminum or magnesium filings or powder
(no coarser than granulated sugar).

Any one of the following oxidizing agents: sodium
dichromate, potassium permanganate, potassium nitrate, or potassium dichromate (no
coarser than granulated sugar).

Container with tight-fitting lid.

c. Preparation.

(1) Using a clean, dry spoon, place one of the
metal powders or filings in the container to
one-third container volume. If metal filings
are used, they should be free of grease.

(2) Wipe the spoon with a clean, dry cloth and
add an equal quantity of one of the above
oxidizing agents.

(3) Tighten the lid on the mixing container, turn
the container on its side and slowly roll until
the two powders are completely mixed. The
mixture is now ready to use and may be
stored for months in this tightly sealed container.

d. Application.

(1) To use this subigniter, spread the material to a depth of at least $\frac{1}{4}$ inch on the
top surface of the thermite which is held in
an assembly described under *Application* of
Thermite Incendiary (0307). Spread another
igniter, preferably Sugar-Chlorate (0201) on
top of this subigniter to about the same depth.
Prepare the mixture for ignition with Fuse
Cord (0101) or Improvised String Fuse
(0102) in the normal manner. The fuse cord
should terminate near the center of the igniter

mixture. The fuse cord initiates the sugar-chlorate igniter which ignites the thermite subigniter which then ignites the thermite.

(2) For delay times longer than those conveniently obtained with fuse cord in ignition of thermite by this subigniter method, refer to chapter 5.

Caution: **Never attempt to ignite thermite subigniter without at least a few seconds delay fuse. It burns extremely fast and hot, and the user could be seriously burned if he were too close when ignition occurred.**

CHAPTER 4
INCENDIARY MATERIALS

0301. NAPALM

a. *Description.*

(1) This item consists of a liquid fuel which is gelled by the addition of soap powder or soap chips. It is easily prepared from readily available materials.

(2) This incendiary can be directly initiated by a match flame. However, if delay is required, the incendiary can be reliably initiated by a delay system consisting of any igniter listed in chapter 3 coupled with a delay mechanisms found in chapter 5.

(3) Napalm incendiary is easily ignited and long burning, and is suitable for setting fire to large wooden structures and other large combustible targets. It adheres to objects, even on vertical surfaces.

b. *Material and Equipment.*

Soap powder or chips (bar soap can be easily shaved or chipped). Detergents *cannot* be used.

Any of the following liquid hydrocarbon fuels: gasoline, fuel oil, diesel oil, kerosene, turpentine, benzol or benzene, toloul or toluene.

A double boiler made from any material with the upper pot having a capacity of at least two quarts.

A spoon or stick for stirring.

A source of heat such as a stove or hot plate.

A knife or grater if only bar soap is available.

An air-tight container.

2. Preparation.

(1) Fill bottom of double boiler with water and heat until the water boils. Shut off source of heat.

(2) Place upper pot on top of bottom pot and remove both containers to a point several feet from the heat source.

(3) Pour soap chips or powder into the upper pot of the double boiler to one-quarter of pot volume.

(4) Pour any one of the liquid hydrocarbon fuels listed under *Material and Equipment* above into the upper pot containing the soap chips or powder until the pot is one-half full.

Caution: **Keep these fuels away from open flames.**

(5) Stir the mixture with a stick or spoon until it thickens to a paste having the consistency of jam. Do this in a well ventilated room where the vapors will not concentrate and burn or explode from a flame or spark.

(6) If the mixture has not thickened enough after about 15 minutes of stirring, remove the upper pot and put it several feet from the heat source. Again bring the water in the lower pot to a boil. Shut off heat source, place upper pot in lower pot at a location several feet from the heat source and repeat stirring until the napalm reaches the recommended consistency.

(7) When the proper consistency is obtained, store the finished napalm in a tightly sealed container until used. Napalm will keep for months when stored this way.

d. Application.

(1) To use napalm most effectively, it should be spread out over the surface of the material to be burned. This will start a large area burning at once. A match can be used to directly initiate this incendiary. A short time delay in ignition can be obtained by combining Fuse Cord (0101) or Improvised String Fuse (0102) and one of the igniter mixtures found in chapter 3. (For example, several spoonfuls of Sugar-Chlorate mixture (0201) are placed in a nonabsorbent wrapping material. Fuse cord is buried in the center of the igniter mixture and the fuse is taped to the wrapping material. This assembly is placed directly on the napalm. Delay times are determined by the length of fuse. Suitable delay mechanisms are given in chapter 5 for delay times longer than those practical with fuse cord.)

(2) Napalm made with the more volatile fuels should not ordinarily be used with a delay longer than one hour because the liquid fuel evaporates and this can reduce its effectiveness. In very hot weather, or if the napalm is exposed to the direct rays of the sun, it is recommended that napalm be made with fuel oil. In extremely cold weather, it is recommended that napalm be made with gasoline.

(3) The destructive effect of napalm is increased when charcoal is added. The charcoal will

readily ignite and the persistent fire from the charcoal will outlast the burning napalm. It is recommended that at least one quart of napalm be used to ignite heavy wooden structures and large wooden sections. A minimum of one-half quart is recommended for wooden structures of small cross section.

0302. GELLED GASOLINE (EXOTIC THICKENERS)

a. Description.

(1) This item consists of gasoline which is gelled with small quantities of organic chemicals. The operation is carried out quickly, without heat, by addition of the chemicals while stirring.

(2) This incendiary can be directly initiated by a match flame. However, any igniter listed in chapter 3 can be used in conjunction with specific delay mechanisms found in chapter 5 for delayed ignition of this incendiary.

(3) Gelled gasoline incendiary is readily ignited, long burning, and is suitable for setting fire to large wooden structures and other large combustible targets. It adheres to objects, even on vertical surfaces.

b. Material and Equipment.

Gasoline.
Balance or scale.
Spoon or stick for stirring.
Large air-tight container.
Small jar.

One of the following seven additive systems:

Components	Grams added per gal gas	Trade name	Manufacturer
SYSTEM 1			
A__ Lauryl amine__	55__	Alamine 4D Formonyte 616 Armeen.	General Mills Foremost Chemical Armour Chemical.
B__ Toluene diiso- cyanate.	27__	Hylene TM–65 Nacconate 65.	DuPont National Aniline.
SYSTEM 2			
A__ Coco amine____	55__	Alamine 21 Formonyte 601.	General Mills Foremost Chemical.
B__ Toluene diiso- cyanate.	27__	Hylene TM–65 Nacconate 65.	DuPont National Aniline.
SYSTEM 3			
A__ Lauryl amine__	57__	Alamine 4D Formonyte 616 Armeen.	General Mills Foremost Chemical Armour Chemical.
B__ Hexamethyl- ene diiso- cyanate.	25__	Hexamethyl- ene diiso- cyanate.	Borden Chemical
SYSTEM 4			
A__ Oleyl amine____	59__	Alamine II Formonyte 608.	General Mills Foremost Chemical.
B__ Hexamethyl- ene diiso- cyanate.	23__	Hexamethyl- ene diiso- cyanate.	Borden Chemical
SYSTEM 5			
A__ t-Octyl amine__	51__	t-Octyl_____	Rohm and Haas
B__ Toluene diiso- cyanate.	31__	Hylene TM–65 Nacconate 65.	DuPont National Aniline.

Components	Grams added per gal gas	Trade name	Manufacturer
SYSTEM 6			
A__ Coco amine____	51__	Alamine 21 Formonyte 601.	General Mills Foremost Chemical.
B__ Naphthyl iso-cyanate.	31__	Naphthyl iso-cyanate.	Distillation Products Industry.
SYSTEM 7			
A__ Delta-amino-butylmethyl-diethoxy-silane.	51__	Delta silane____	Union Carbide
B__ Hexamethyl-ene diiso-cyanate.	31__	Hexamethyl-ene diiso-cyanate.	Borden Chemical

c. *Preparation.*

(1) Determine the amount of gasoline to be gelled and place this amount in the large container.

Caution: **Keep this material away from open flames.**

(2) Weigh out the appropriate quantity of component A. This can be calculated by multiplying the number of gallons of gasoline by the figure given in the *Grams Added Per Gal. Gas.* column of systems. (For example, if System 1 is being used and five gallons of gasoline are being gelled, then (5×55) or 275 grams of Lauryl amine are required).

(3) Add component A to the gasoline and stir for a few minutes to dissolve.

Caution: **Both components A and B are corrosive to the skin. If any of these materials contact the skin, wash the area with detergent and water.**

(4) Clean the small container used to weight component A thoroughly or use another container for weighing component B. Weigh out the proper quantity of component B. Calculate the proper amount as mentioned above for component A.

(5) Stir the gasoline—component A mixture rapidly and add all of component B at once, not a little at a time. At the same time that component B enters the mixture, remove the stirring rod and allow a few minutes for the gelling to take place.

(6) Store the gelled gasoline in a tightly sealed container until ready to use. It will keep for months when stored in this manner.

d. Application.

(1) To use gelled gasoline most effectively, it should be spread out over the surface of the material to be burned. This will start a large area burning at once. A match can be used to directly initiate this incendiary. A short time delay in ignition can be obtained by combining Fuse Cord (0101), or Improvised String Fuse (0102) and one of the igniter mixtures found in chapter 3. (For example, several spoonfuls of Sugar-Chlorate Mixture (0201) are placed in a nonabsorbent wrapping material. Fuse cord is buried in the center of the igniter mixture and the fuse is taped to the wrapping material. This assembly is placed directly on the gelled

gasoline. Delay times are determined by the length of fuse. Suitable delay mechanisms are given in chapter 5 for delay times longer than those practical with fuse cord.)

(2) Gelled gasoline should not ordinarily be used with a delay longer than one hour because gasoline evaporates and this can reduce its effectiveness.

(3) The destructive effect of gelled gasoline is increased when charcoal is added. The charcoal will readily ignite and the persistent fire from the charcoal will outlast the burning gasoline. It is recommended that at least one quart of gelled gasoline be used to ignite heavy wooden structures and large wooden sections. A minimum of one-half quart is recommended for wooden structures of small cross section.

Note. All of the chemicals used for the gelling process *must* be added in a *liquid* state. Many of the chemicals solidify at near freezing temperatures (32° F.) and uniform gels are difficult to produce at these temperatures.

0303. GELLED GASOLINE (IMPROVISED THICKENERS)
0303.1 LYE SYSTEMS

(1) This item consists of gasoline which is gelled by the addition of certain ingredients that are locally available. The following eight basic systems will produce gelled gasoline and are easily prepared: Lye systems, Lye-alcohol systems, Lye-balsam systems, Soap-alcohol systems, Egg system, Latex system, Wax systems, and Animal blood systems. These systems are discussed in the subparagraphs under 0303.

(2) These incendiaries can be directly initiated by a match flame. However, any igniter listed in chapter 3 can be used in conjunction with specific delay mechanisms given in chapter 5 for delayed ignition.

(3) Gelled gasoline incendiary is readily ignited, long burning and is suitable for setting fire to large wooden structures and other large combustible targets. It adheres to objects, even on vertical surfaces.

b. Material and Equipment.

Ingredient	Parts by volume	Used for	Common source
Gasoline__	60_____	Motor fuel_____	Gas stations or motor vehicles.
Lye_____	2 (flake) or 1 (powder).	Drain cleaner, making of soap, etc.	Food and drug stores, soap factories.
Water____	1 or 2____	(Always use about same amount as dry lye).	
Rosin powder.	15_____	Paint or varnish, Naval supply, industrial uses.	Food and drug stores, pine tree extract, pai..t and varnish factories.

Two air-tight containers
Spoon or stick for stirring

Note. Lye is also known as caustic soda or sodium hydroxide. Allow for strength of lye; if only 50% (as in Drano), use twice the amount indicated above. Castor oil can be substituted for the rosin. Potassium hydroxide (caustic potash, potassa) may be used in place of lye.

c. Preparation.

(1) Measure the required quantity of gasoline and place in a clean container.

Caution: **Keep material away from open flames.**

(2) Break the rosin into *small* pieces and add to the gasoline.

(3) Stir the mixture for about five minutes to disperse the rosin.

(4) In a separate container dissolve the lye in water.

Caution: **Add lye to water slowly. Do not prepare this solution in an aluminum container.**

(5) Add this solution to the gasoline mixture and stir until mixture thickens (about one minute).

(6) The mixture will thicken to a very firm butter paste within cne to two days. The mixture can be thinned, if desired, by mixing in additional gasoline. Store in an air-tight container until ready to use.

d. Alternate Preparation Using Pyrethrum Extract Instead of Rosin.

(1) Replace rosin by the following:

Ingredient	Parts by volume	Used for	Common source
Pyrethrum extract (20%).	18_____	Insecticide, medicine.	Hardware stores, garden supply, drug stores.

(2) Measure 78 parts by volume of gasoline and place in a clean container.

Caution: **Keep material away from open flames.**

(3) Dissolve the pyrethrum extract in the gasoline by stirring.

(4) In another container dissolve the lye in water.

Caution: **Add lye to water slowly. Do not prepare this solution in an aluminum container.**

(5) Add 4 parts by volume of the lye solution to the gasoline mixture.

(6) Stir every 15 minutes until gel forms. Store in an air-tight container until ready to use.

e. *Application*

(1) To use gelled gasoline most effectively, it should be spread out over the surface of the material to be burned. This will start a large area burning at once. A match can be used to directly initiate this incendiary. A short time delay in ignition can be obtained by combining Fuse Cord (0101) or Improvised String Fuse (0102) and one of the igniter mixtures found in chapter 3. (For example, several spoonfuls of Sugar-Chlorate Mixture (0201) are placed in a nonabsorbent wrapping material. Fuse cord is buried in the center of the igniter mixture and the fuse is taped to the wrapping material. This assembly is placed directly on the gelled gasoline. Delay times are determined by the length of fuse. Suitable delay mechanisms are given in chapter 5 for delay times longer than those practical with fuse cord.)

(2) Gelled gasoline should not ordinarily be used with a delay longer than one hour because gasoline evaporates and this can reduce its effectiveness.

(3) The destructive effect of gelled gasoline is increased when charcoal is added. The charcoal will readily ignite and the persistent

fire from the charcoal will outlast the burning gasoline. It is recommended that at least one quart of gelled gasoline be used to ignite heavy wooden structures and large wooden sections. A minimum of one-half quart is recommended for wooden structures of small cross section.

0303.2 LYE-ALCOHOL SYSTEMS

a. Description. See Paragraph 0303.1.

b. Material and Equipment.

Ingredient	Parts by volume	Used for	Common source
Gasoline__	58_____	Motor fuel_____	Gas stations or motor vehicles.
Lye_____	2 (flake) or 1 (powder).	Drain cleaner, making of soap.	Food and drug stores, soap factories.
Water____	1 or 2____	(Always use about the same amount as dry lye).	
Ethyl alcohol.	3_____	Whiskey_____	Liquor stores.
Tallow___	14_____	Food_____	Fat extracted from solid fat or suet of cattle, sheep, or horses.

Spoon or stick for stirring
Two air-tight containers

Note. Lye is also known as caustic soda or sodium hydroxide. Allow for strength of lye. If only 50% (as in Drano), use twice the amount indicated above. Methyl (wood) alcohol, isopropyl (rubbing) alcohol or antifreeze product can be substituted for whiskey, but their use produces softer gels. Potassium hydroxide (caustic potash, potassa) may be used in place of lye.

(1) The following can be substituted for the tallow in order of preference:

    (*a*) Wool grease (lanolin) (very good)—fat extracted from sheep wool.

    (*b*) Castor oil (good).

    (*c*) Any vegetable oil (corn, cottonseed, peanut, linseed, etc.).

    (*d*) Any fish oil.

    (*e*) Butter or oleo margarine.

(2) When using substitutes (1)(*c*) and (*e*) above, it will be necessary to double the recommended amount of fat and of the lye solution for satisfactory thickening.

c. Preparation.

(1) Measure out the appropriate amount of gasoline and place in a clean container.

Caution: Keep material away from open flames.

(2) Add the tallow to the gasoline and stir for about one-half minute to dissolve the tallow.

(3) Add the alcohol to the mixture.

(4) In another container dissolve the lye in water.

Caution: Add lye to water slowly. Do not prepare this solution in an aluminum container.

(5) Add the lye solution to the gasoline mixture and stir occasionally until the mixture thickens (about one-half hour).

(6) The mixture will thicken to a very firm butter paste in one to two days. The mixture can be thinned, if desired, by mixing in additional gasoline. Store in an air-tight container until ready to use.

d. Application. See paragraph 0303.1.

TAGO 7189-C

0303.3 LYE-BALSAM SYSTEMS

a. Description. See paragraph 0303.1.

b. Material and Equipment.

Ingredient	Parts by volume	Used for	Common source
Gasoline__	80_____	Motor fuel_____	Gas stations or . motor vehicles:
Either: Copaiba balsam Copaiba resin Jesuits' balsam.	14_____	Medicine, varnish, odor fixative.	Drug stores, varnish factories, perfume processors, natural oleoresin.
Or: Tolu balsam Tolu resin Thomas balsam.	14_____	Medicine, perfume, confectionery, fumigant, chewing gum.	Drug stores, perfume processors, candy manufacturers.
Lye_____	3_____	Drain cleaner, making of soap.	Food and drug stores, soap factories.

Water____ 3
Spoon or stick for stirring
Two air-tight containers

Note. Lye is also known as caustic soda or sodium hydroxide. Allow for the strength of the lye. If only 50% (as in Drano), use twice the amount indicated above. Potassium hydroxide (caustic potash, potassa) may be used in place of lye.

c. Preparation.

(1) Dissolve the lye in water using a clean container.

Caution: **Add lye to water slowly. Do not prepare this solution in an aluminum container.**

(2) Stir gasoline and copaiba balsam in another clean container.

(3) Add the saturated lye solution to the gasoline mixture and stir until the gel forms. Store in an air-tight container until ready to use.

Note. Increase the lye solution to 10 parts by volume (5 parts lye, 5 parts water) if the gasoline does not thicken.

d. *Application.* See paragraph 0303.1.

0303.4 SOAP-ALCOHOL SYSTEMS

a. *Description.* See paragraph 0303.1.

b. *Material and Equipment.*

Ingredient	Parts by volume	Used for	Common source
Gasoline__	36_____	Motor fuel_____	Gas stations or motor vehicles.
Ethyl alcohol.	1_____	Whiskey_____	Liquor stores
Laundry soap.	20 (powder) or 28 (flake).	Washing_____	Food stores

Air-tight container
Spoon or stick for stirring

Note. Methyl (wood) or isoprophyl (rubbing) alcohols can be substituted for the ethyl alcohol. When a stronger alcohol (150 proof) or one of the dry alcohol substitutes is used, add an amount of water to make the concentration 50% by volume. (The *percent* alcohol is equal to $\frac{1}{2}$ of the *proof*—150 proof is 75% alcohol.)

(1) Unless the word *soap* actually appears somewhere on the container or wrapper (at retail store level), a washing compound may be assumed to be a synthetic detergent. Soaps

react with mineral salts in hard water to form a sticky insoluble scum while synthetic detergents do not. Synthetic detergents cannot be used.

(2) The following is a list of commercially available soap products (at retail store level):

Name	Manufacturer
Ivory Snow	Proctor and Gamble
Ivory Flakes	Proctor and Gamble
Lux Flakes	Lever Brothers
Chiffon Flakes	Armour
Palmolive Bar Soap	Colgate-Palmolive
Sweetheart Bar Soap	Manhattan Soap Company
Octagon Bar Soap	Colgate-Palmolive

(3) Home prepared bar soaps may be used in place of purchased bar soaps.

c. *Preparation.*

(1) Measure out the appropriate amount of gasoline and place in a clean container.

Caution: **Keep material away from open flames.**

(2) Add the alcohol to the gasoline.

(3) Add the soap powder to the gasoline-alcohol mixture, and stir occasionally until the mixture thickens (about 15 minutes).

(4) The mixture will thicken to a very firm butter paste in one to two days. It can be thinned, if desired, by mixing in additional gasoline. Store in an air-tight container until ready to use.

d. *Application.* See paragraph 0303.1.

65

0303.5 EGG SYSTEM

a. *Description.* See paragraph 0303.1.

b. *Material and Equipment.*

Ingredient	Parts by volume	Chemical name	Used for	Common source
Gasoline	85		Motor fuel	Gas stations or motor vehicles.
Egg whites (chicken, ostrich, duck, turtle, etc.).	14		Food, industrial processes.	Food stores, farms.
Use any one of the following additives:				
Table salt	1	Sodium chloride	Food, industrial processes.	Sea water, natural brine, food stores.
Ground coffee (not decaffeinized).	3		Beverage	Food stores, coffee processors.
Leaf tea	3		Beverage	Cacao trees, food stores.
Sugar	2	Sucrose	Sweetening foods, industrial processes.	Sugar cane, food stores.
Borax	2	Sodium tetraborate decahydrate.	Washing aid, industrial processes.	Natural in some areas, food stores.
Saltpeter (Niter).	1	Potassium nitrate.	Pyrotechnics, explosives, matches, medicine.	Natural deposits, drug stores.

Ingredient	Parts by volume	Chemical name	Used for	Common source
Epsom salts__	1___	Mganesium sulfate hepta- hydrate.	Medicine, mineral water, industrial processes.	Natural deposits, Kieserite, drug and food stores.
Washing soda (sal soda).	2___	Sodium carbon- ate deca- hydrate.	Washing cleanser, medicine, photog- raphy.	Food, drug, and photo supply stores.
Baking soda__	2___	Sodium bicar- bonate.	Baking ef- fervescent salts, beverages, mineral waters, medicine, industrial processes.	Food and drug stores.
Aspirin (crushed).	2___	Acetylsali- cylic acid.	Medicine____	Food and drug stores.

Spoon or stick for stirring
Two air-tight containers

c. Preparation.

(1) Separate the egg white from the yolk as follows:

(a) *Method 1.* Crack the egg at approximately the center. Allow the egg white to drain into a clean container. When most of the egg white has drained off, flip the yellow egg yolk from one-half shell to the other, each time allowing the egg white to drain into the container. Transfer the egg white to a capped jar for storage or directly into the container being used for the gelled flame fuel. Discard the egg yolk. Repeat the process with each egg. Do not get the yellow egg yolk mixed into the egg white. If egg yolk gets into the egg white, discard the egg.

(b) *Method 2.* Crack the egg and transfer (CAREFULLY SO AS TO AVOID BREAKING THE YOLK) the egg to a shallow dish. Tilt the dish slowly and pour off the egg white into a suitable container while holding back the yellow egg yolk with a flat piece of wood, knife blade, or fingers. Transfer the egg white to a capped jar for storage or directly to the container being used for the gelled flame fuel. Discard the egg yolk. Repeat the process with each egg being careful not to get yellow egg yolk mixed in with the egg white. If egg yolk gets into egg white, discard the egg and wash the dish.

(2) Store egg white in an ice box, refrigerator, cave, cold running stream, or other cool area until ready to prepare the gelled flame fuel.

(3) Pour the egg white into a clean container.

(4) Add the gasoline.

Caution: **Keep material away from open flames.**

(5) Add the table salt (or one of its substitutes) and stir until the gel forms (about 5–10 minutes). Use within 24 hours. Thicker gelled flame fuels can be obtained by—

(a) Reducing the gasoline content to 80 parts by volume (NO LOWER); or

(b) Putting the capped jars in hot (65° C., 149° F.) water for ½ hour and then letting them cool tờ ambient temperature. (DO NOT HEAT THE GELLED FUEL CONTAINING COFFEE.)

d. *Application.* See paragraph 0303.1.

0303.6 LATEX SYSTEM

a. *Description.* See paragraph 0303.1.

b. *Material and Equipment.*

Ingredient	Parts by volume	Used for	Common source
Gasoline	92	Motor fuel	Gas stations or motor vehicles.
Either:			
Latex commercial or natural.	7	Paints, adhesives, rubber products.	Natural from tree or plant, rubber cement, general stores.
Or:			
Guayule Gutta percha Balata.	7	Wire insulation, waterproofing, machinery belts, golf ball covers, gaskets.	Coagulated and dried latex, rubber industry.
Any one of the following:			
Dilute acetic acid (vinegar).	1	Salad dressing, developing photographic films.	Food stores, fermented apple cider or wine, photography supply.
Sulfuric acid, battery acid (oil of vitriol).	1	Storage batteries, material processing.	Motor vehicles, industrial plants.
Hydrochloric acid 1 (muriatic acid).	1	Petroleum wells, pickling and metal cleaning, industrial processes.	Hardware stores, industrial plants.

Air-tight container
Spoon or stick for stirring

Caution: **Sulfuric acid and hydrochloric acid will burn skin and ruin clothing. The fumes will irritate nose passages, lungs and eyes. Wash with large quantities of water upon contact.**

c. *Preparation.*

    (1) Commercial rubber latex may be used without further treatments before adding it to gasoline.

    (2) Natural rubber latex will coagulate (form lumps) as it comes from the plant. Strain off the thick part for use in flame fuel. If the rubber latex does not form lumps, add a small amount of acid to coagulate the latex and use the rubbery lump for gelling. It is best to air-dry the wet lumps before adding them to gasoline.

    (a) *Using commercial rubber latex.*

        1. Place the latex and the gasoline in the container to be used for the gelled gasoline and stir.

Caution: **Keep material away from open flames.**

        2. Add the vinegar (or other acid) to the liquid in the container and stir again until the gel forms. Store in an air-tight container until ready to use.

    Note. Use gelled gasoline as soon as possible because it becomes thinner on standing. If the gel is too thin, reduce the gasoline content (but not below 85% by volume).

        3. Natural rubber latex coagulates readily. If acids are not available, use one volume of acid salt (alum, sulfates and chlorides other than sodium and potassium). The formic acid content of crushed red ants will coagulate natural rubber latex.

(b) *Using natural rubber latex.*

80 parts by volume of gasoline.

20 parts by volume of coagulated or dried rubber.

Let the rubber lump soak in the gasoline in a closed container two or three days until a gelled mass is obtained. Prepare the gelled gasoline using the above formulation. This gelled gasoline should be used as soon as possible after it has thickened sufficiently.

d. *Application.* See paragraph 0303.1.

0303.7 WAX SYSTEMS

a. *Description.* See paragraph 0303.1.

b. *Material and Equipment.*

Ingredient	Parts by volume	Used for	Common source
Gasoline	80	Motor fuel	Gas stations or motor vehicles.
Any one of the following waxes:			
Ozocerite mineral wax fossil wax ceresin wax.	20	Leather polish, sealing wax, candles crayons, waxed paper, textile sizing.	Natural deposits, general and department stores.
Beeswax	20	Furniture and floor waxes, artificial fruit and flowers, wax paper, candles.	Honeycomb from bees, general and department stores.

Ingredient	Part by volume	Used for	Common source
Bayberry wax myrtle wax.	20_ _	Candles, soaps, leather polish, medicine.	Natural from myrica berries, general, department, and drug stores.
Lye_ _ _ _ _ _ _ _ _ _ _	0.5_	Drain cleaner, making of soap.	Food and drug stores, soap factories.

Two air-tight containers
Spoon or stick for stirring

Caution: Lye causes severe burns to eyes.

Note. Lye is also known as caustic soda or sodium hydroxide. Allow for strength of lye. If only 50% (as in Drano), use twice the amount indicated above. Potassium hydroxide (caustic potash, potassa) may be used in place of lye.

c. *Preparation.*

  (1) *Wax from natural sources.*

  (a) Plants and berries are potential sources of natural waxes. Place the plants and/or berries in boiling water. The natural waxes will melt. Let the water cool, and the natural waxes will form a solid layer on the water surface. Skim off the wax and let it dry.

  (b) Natural waxes which have suspended matter should be melted and screened through a cloth.

  (2) *Gel from gasoline and wax.*

  (a) Put the gasoline in a clean container.

Caution: Keep material away from open flames.

(b) Melt the wax and pour it into the gasoline container.

(c) Tightly cap the container and place it in hot water (sufficiently hot so that a small piece of wax will melt on the surface).

(d) When the wax has dissolved in the gasoline, place the capped container in a warm water bath and permit it to cool slowly to air temperature.

(e) If a solid paste of gel does not form, add another 10 parts by volume of melted wax and repeat (b), (c), and (d) above.

(f) Continue adding wax (up to 40 parts by volume) as before until a paste or gel is formed. If no paste forms at 80 parts by volume of gasoline and 40 parts by volume of melted wax, the wax is not satisfactory for gelled gasolines and may be used only in combination with alkali.

(3) *Gel from gasoline, wax and alkali.*
    70 parts by volume of gasoline
    29.5 parts by volume of melted wax
    0.5 parts by volume of staurated lye solution

(a) Prepare the saturated lye solution by *carefully adding one volume of lye* (or two volumes of Drano) to one volume of water and stir with a glass rod or wooden stick until the lye is dissolved.

Caution: **Lye causes severe burns to eyes. Add the lye to the water slowly. Let cool to room temperature and pour off the saturated liquid solution. Do not prepare this solution in an aluminum container.**

73

(b) Prepare the gasoline-wax solution according to the method described above.

(c) After the solution has cooled for about 15 minutes, CAUTIOUSLY loosen the cap, remove it and add the saturated lye solution.

(d) Stir about every five minutes until a gel forms. If the gel is not thick enough, remelt with another 5 parts by volume of wax and 0.1 part by volume of saturated lye solution. Stir contents as before. Store in an airtight container until ready to use.

Note. In addition to the listed waxes, the following may be used: candelilla wax, carnauba (Brazil) wax, Chinese (insect) wax, Japan (sumac) wax, montan (lignite) wax, and palm wax.

d. *Application.* See paragraph 0303.1.

0303.8 ANIMAL BLOOD SYSTEMS

a. *Description.* See paragraph 0303.1.

b. *Material and Equipment.*

Ingredient	Parts by volume	Chemical name	Used for	Common source
Gasoline	68		Motor fuel	Gas stations or motor vehicles.
Animal blood (sheep, cow, hog, dog, etc.).	30		Food, medicine.	Slaughter houses, natural habitat.
Any one of the following:				
Coffee (not decaffeinized).	2		Food, caffeine source, beverage.	Coffee processors, food stores.
Leaf tea	2		Food, beverage.	Tea processors, food stores.

Ingredient	Parts by volume	Chemical name	Used for	Common source
Lime_____	2___	Calcium oxide.	Mortar, plaster, medicine, ceramics, industrial processes.	From calcium carbonate, hardware and drug stores.
Baking soda	2___	Sodium bi-carbon--ate.	Baking, beverages, medicine, industrial processes.	Food and drug stores.
Epsom salts.	2___	Magnesium sulfate hepta-hydrate.	Medicine, industrial processes, mineral water.	Natural deposits, drug and food stores.

Two air-tight containers
Spoon or stick for stirring

   c. Preparation.

      (1) *Animal blood serum.*

         (a) Slit animal's throat by jugular vein. Hang upside down to drain.

         (b) Place coagulated (lumpy) blood in a cloth or on a screen and catch the red fluid (serum) which drains through.

         (o) Store in a cool place if possible.

   Caution: **Animal blood can cause infections. Do not get aged animal blood or the serum into an open cut.**

      (2) *Preparation of gelled gasoline.*

         (a) Pour the animal bolod serum into a clean container and add the gasoline.

   Caution: **Keep material away from open flames.**

     (*b*) Add the lime and stir the mixture for a few minutes until a firm gel forms. Store in an air-tight container until ready to use.

> *Note.* Egg white may be substituted for up to ½ of the animal blood serum.

d. Application. See paragraph 0303.1.

0304. PARAFFIN-SAWDUST

a. Description.

    (1) This item consists of a mixture of paraffin wax and sawdust. It is easily prepared and safe to carry. It is used to ignite wooden structures including heavy beams and timbers. It will also ignite paper, rags and other tinder type materials to build larger fires.

    (2) This incendiary can be safely ignited by a match flame. However, any igniter listed in chapter 3 can be used in conjunction with specific delay mechanisms in chapter 5 for delayed ignition of this incendiary.

    (3) All or part of the paraffin wax may be replaced by beeswax but *not* by vegetable or animal fats or greases.

b. Material and Equipment.

Paraffin wax, beeswax, or wax obtained by melting candles.

Sawdust.

Source of heat (stove, hot plate).

Pot.

Spoon or stick for stirring.

c. Preparation.

    (1) Put enough wax in the pot so that it is about half full.

(2) Heat the pot on a stove or hot plate until the wax melts.

(3) Remove the heated pot from the stove or hot plate and shut off the source of heat. Add the sawdust to the melted wax until the pot is nearly full. Stir the mixture with a spoon or stick for a few minutes, being sure there is no layer of wax at the bottom of the pot which has not been mixed with the sawdust.

(4) While the mixture is in a fluid state, pour it into a waxed paper carton or other container. Upon cooling, the wax mixture will harden and take the shape of the container. The mixture can be stored for months without losing its effectiveness. If it becomes wet, it will be effective again when it is dried.

(5) A less effective incendiary may be made by melting some paraffin or beeswax, dipping sheets of paper in the molten wax for a few seconds, and removing the paper to let the wax harden. This waxed paper lights readily from a match. Although not as hot or persistent or the paraffin-sawdust mixture, the waxed paper is an excellent incendiary and may be substituted in many instances for initiating readily ignitable materials. The paper may be wadded up, folded, or torn into strips.

d. *Application.*

(1) Place about a quart of the mixture in a paper bag and put the bag down on the object to be burned. A match may be used to ignite the bag which will then ignite the paraffin-sawdust mixture. The fire starts very slowly so there

is no hazard involved, and it usually takes two or three minutes before the paraffin-sawdust mixture is burning strongly. This, of course, is a disadvantage where a hot fire is required quickly. Once started, however, this mixture burns vigorously because the paraffin itself gives a fairly hot flame and the sawdust acts like charcoal to increase the destructive effect.

(2) Where very large wooden beams or structures are to be burned use more of the mixture. A bag containing two or three quarts will be enough to set fire to almost any object on which paraffin-sawdust mixture can be used effectively.

(3) To be most effective on wood structures, this mixture should be in a pile, *never* spread out in a thin layer. If possible, place it under the object. When placing the incendiary in a packing box or in a room, place it in a corner.

0305. FIRE-BOTTLE (IMPACT IGNITION)

a. Description.

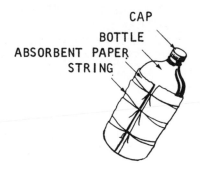

This item consists of a glass bottle containing gasoline and concentrated sulfuric acid. The exterior of the bottle is wrapped with a rag or absorbent paper. Just before use, the rag is soaked with a saturated solution of granulated sugar and potassium chlorate. Thrown against hard-surfaced targets such as tanks, automotive vehicles or railroad boxcars, this fire bottle is a very effective incendiary.

    b. Material and Equipment.

Concentrated sulfuric acid (para 0103).

Gasoline.

Potassium chlorate (powdered).

Sugar (granulated).

Jar or bottle, with cap or stopper (½ pint).

Cloth or absorbent paper.

Jar or bottle, with cap or stopper (1 quart).

String or tape.

Heat resistant glass or porcelain pot (1 pint capacity).

Heat source.

Glass funnel.

Spoon.

Small container for measuring.

    c. Preparation.

(1) Using the funnel, pour the gasoline into the quart bottle until approximately two thirds full.

Caution: Keep this material away from open flames.

(2) Slowly add concentrated sulfuric acid through the funnel to the gasoline in the bottle and fill the bottle to within one inch of the top. The funnel must be used to direct the concentrated acid into the gasoline in the center

of the bottle. Stopper or cap the bottle securely.

Note. If only battery-grade sulfuric acid is available, it must be concentrated. See instructions under paragraph 0103.

(3) Flush the tightly capped bottle with water to remove any gasoline or acid adhering to the outside surface and dry the bottle. This *must* be done to avoid accidental combustion during the following steps.

(4) Wrap a clean cloth or several sheets of absorbent paper around the bottle. Fasten with strings or rubber bands.

(5) Prepare a saturated solution of granulated sugar and potassium chlorate in water as directed below.

(6) Add six measures of water to the porcelain pot and dry the measuring container with a clean rag or paper towel.

(7) Bring the water to a boil.

(8) Using a clean, dry spoon, place granulated sugar in the measuring container and add one and one-half measures of sugar to the boiling water.

(9) Wipe the spoon with a clean rag or paper towel and place one measure of potassium chlorate into the boiling sugar water.

(10) Remove the pot of boiling mixture immediately from the heat source and shut off heat source.

(11) When the solution is cool, pour it into the small ½ pint bottle using the glass funnel and cap tightly.

(12) Flush this bottle with water to remove any solution or crystals adhering to the outside surface and dry the bottle. When the crystals settle, there should be about ⅓ liquid above the crystals.

Caution: Store this bottle separately from the other bottle containing gasoline and concentrated sulfuric acid.

d. *Application.*

(1) Just prior to actual use, shake the bottle containing the sugar-potassium chlorate crystals and pour onto the cloth or paper wrapped around the gasoline-acid bottle. The fire bottle can be used while the cloth is still wet or

after it has dried. However when dry, the sugar-potassium chlorate mixture is very sensitive to sparks, open flame, bumping and scraping. In the dry condition the bottle should be handled carefully.

(2) The fire bottle should be gripped in one hand and thrown like a hand grenade. Upon impact with a metallic or other hard surface, the bottle will break and the sugar-potassium chlorate will react with the sulfuric acid. This reaction ignites the gasoline which will engulf the target area in flames.

0306. FIRE BOTTLE (DELAY IGNITION)

a. Description.

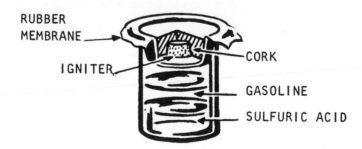

RUBBER MEMBRANE

IGNITER

CORK

GASOLINE

SULFURIC ACID

(1) This item consists of a bottle of gasoline and concentrated sulfuric acid which is ignited by the chemical reaction of the acid with Sugar-Chlorate Igniter (0201). A delay feature is incorporated in this incendiary. The amount of delay is determined by time it takes the sulfuric acid to corrode a rubber membrane and react with the igniter mix. Immediate ignition may also be achieved by breaking the bottle and allowing the ingredients to mix.

(2) Prepared fire bottles are stored upright. This allows the heavier acid to lay on the bottom, with the gasoline on top. When put in use, the bottle is inverted, allowing the acid to come in contact with the rubber membrane and to begin corroding it.

b. *Material and Equipment.*

Wide mouth bottle.
Cork or rubber stopper (must fit snugly in bottle).
Sheet rubber on rubber membrane.
Sugar-Chlorate Igniter (0201).
Concentrated Sulfuric Acid (0103).
Gasoline.

c. *Preparation*

(1) Cut or drill a cavity on the bottom of the cork big enough to hold at least two teaspoonfuls of sugar-chlorate igniter. Be careful not to break through the cork. If the hole does go all the way through, it must be sealed with another smaller cork.

(2) Fill the bottle with a 50/50 concentration of gasoline and sulfuric acid. Pour the gasoline in first, then add the sulfuric acid carefully, making certain not to splash acid on the skin or in the eyes.

Note. If only battery grade sulfuric acid is available it must be concentrated before it can be used. See paragraph 0103 for details of concentration process.

(3) Fill the hole in the cork with Sugar-Chlorate Igniter (0201). Cover the side of the cork containing the igniter with a piece of thin rubber membrane and then force the cork into the gasoline-acid filled bottle. Take care to prevent any of the igniter mix from falling into the jar.

d. *Alternate Method of Preparation.*

(1) Drill or cut a hole all the way through the cork.

(2) Fill the bottle with gasoline and acid as described above.

(3) Place the rubber membrane over the cork and install in the bottle. Make certain that cork is fitted tightly and rubber membrane fully covers the inner portion of the bottle.

(4) Fill the hole in the cork with igniter mixture as before and install a small cork in the hole covering the igniter mixture.

e. *Application.*

(1) To start the delay working invert the bottle. The acid will begin corroding the rubber membrane. When the acid breaks through, it will react violently and either break the bottle or blow out the cork stopper and ignite the gasoline.

(2) The Delay Fire Bottle works well on readily ignited materials where the scattering of the burning gasoline will start a number of fires at once. To ignite wooden structures, preparation such as piling up of flammable tinder and kindling is required.

(3) The delay time for initiation of the gasoline is slowed down in cold weather and may be stopped if the acid freezes. Check the delay time by testing the acid with the identical thickness rubber membrane at the temperature of expected use. Always use concentrated sulfuric acid.

0307. THERMITE

a. *Description.*

(1) Thermite is composed of magnetic iron flakes and aluminum powder. Thermite may be obtained as a manufactured item or may be improvised for use in welding machinery parts together and burning holes in metal structures. The termite reaction is initiated by strong heat and therefore cannot be directly ignited with a safety fuse or match.

The following igniters, found in chapter 3, may be used to initiate thermite: Powdered Aluminum—Sulfur Pellets (0207), Magnesium Powder—Barium Peroxide Igniter (0210), and Subigniter for Thermite (0211).

(2) Thermite is very safe to handle and transport because of its high ignition temperature. It burns well in cold and windy weather. Thermite will penetrate a sealed metal container and ignite the contents. It may be easily improvised if aluminum powder and iron oxide particles of the proper size are available.

b. *Material and Equipment.*

Aluminum powder (no coarser than ground coffee).

Iron oxide flakes (Fe_3O_4—similar to coarse ground coffee).

Spoon or cup for measuring.

Jar or can with tight fitting lid.

Cardboard can with metal ends.

c. *Preparation.*

(1) Place three parts by volume of iron oxide and two parts by volume of aluminum powder into the jar. Leave enough empty space to facilitiate mixing.

(2) Tighten the lid on the jar, turn the jar on its side and slowly roll until the two powders are completely mixed. The mixture is now ready for use and may be stored for months in the sealed container.

d. *Application.*

(1) Thermite is used to attack metallic targets such as transformers, electric motors, file cabinets, gears, bearings, boilers, storage tanks

and pipelines. In operation, the methods described below produce a quantity of molten metal that streams out the bottom of the unit. On contact with the target, the molten metal will cut through the outer metal casing and pour molten metal on the interior. Thermite is *not* recommended for use on moderate or heavy wooden structures or other applications where a persistent flame is required. Two basic techniques are described, one for burning holes in steel and the other for welding steel parts together.

(a) *Burning holes.*

1. In order to penetrate a steel plate with the minimum quantity of thermite, the mass of ignited thermite must be held away from the target during the initial combustion period. This minimizes conductive heat loss (from the thermite to the target) during this period and results in the thermite attaining maximum combustion temperature. When that temperature is reached, the thermite is dropped onto the steel plate surface and a hole is burned through the plate. The following illus trates the method for burning a hole through a plate of ⅜ inch structural steel.

2. Cut a cardboard can (having metal ends) into two equal sections. Example of the type of cardboard container required are which contain household abrasive cleaners such as *AJAX, BON AMI* and *OLD DUTCH CLEANSER.*

3. One section of the can trimmed to a height of 2 inches and two side vents are cut as shown below.

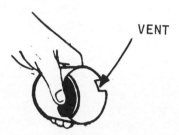

VENT

4. The other section is filled approximately ⅔ full with thermite. The thermite is then completely covered with one of the three above mentioned igniter materials to a depth of at least ¼ inch. Place the end of a length of Fuse Cord (0101) into the igniter mix, making certain that it does not extend into the thermite itself but ends in the center of the igniter mixture. Improvised String Fuse (0102) may be substituted for the Fuse Cord (0101) if desired.

5. The final assembly is constructed by placing the vented section, open face down, over the target area. The metallic end of this section is now facing up, away from the target surface. The section filled with thermite, igniter, and fuse is placed on top of the vented section. Both metal ends of the cardboard can are now touching.

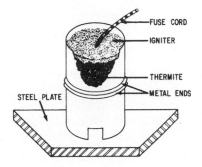

FUSE CORD

IGNITER

THERMITE

METAL ENDS

STEEL PLATE

6. After ignition, the thermite burns a hole through the steel plate dropping extremely hct particles of molten slag into the interior of the steel container. The side vents cut in the bottom section of the can allow excess slag to run off and not close up the hole in the steel target.

(b) *Welding.*

1. A different method is employed when thermite is used to weld machinery components or plates together. The procedure is similar to that used for burning through steel except that the bottom stand-off is eliminated and the amount of thermite can be less than that used to burn through a ⅜ inch steel plate. The assembly is shown below.

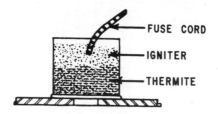

FUSE CORD

IGNITER

THERMITE

2. In this instance, heat is conducted from the
thermite to the steel during the combustion period. Thus, the steel is heated to
nearly the same temperature as the slag
and a weld is effectively made.

Caution: **Never attempt to ignite thermite
without at least a few seconds delay time
because it burns so quickly and so hot that
the user could be seriously burned if he were
nearby when ignition took place.**

0308. FLAMMABLE LIQUIDS

a. Description. Flammable liquids are an excellent
incendiary for starting fires with easily combustible
material. They burn with a hot flame and have many
uses as incendiaries. Most of these liquids are readily
available and they are easily ignited with a match.
However, these liquids tend to flow off the target and
their characteristic odor may cast suspicion on the
person found carrying them.

b. Material and Equipment.
Can or bottle with tight fitting lid (minimum 1
pint capacity).
One of the following volatile liquids:
Gasoline   Cleaners naptha
Kerosene   Turpentine

90

Toluene or Toluol	Lighter fluid
Xylene or Xylol	Fuel oil
Benzene or Benzol	Alcohol

c. Preparation. No preparation other than placing the liquid into an air-tight container for storage and transportation to the target is required.

d. Application. The most effective way to use flammable liquids is to pour at least a pint of the liquid on a pile of rags or sawdust which have been place in a corner of a packing box or other wooden object. This procedure keeps the liquid concentrated in a small area and gives a more persistent flame for igniting wooden objects. If small pieces of charcoal are available, they should be soaked with the flammable liquid and placed on the target. The charcoal will ignite and give a hot, persistent glow that is long lasting. After placing the flammable liquid on the target, throw a lighted match on a soaked area. Do not stand too close when this is done.

0309. INCENDIARY BRICK

a. Description.

(1) This incendiary is composed of potassium chlorate, sulfur, sugar, iron filings and wax. When properly made, it looks like an ordinary building brick and can be easily transported without detection. The incendiary brick will ignite wooden walls, floors, and many other combustible objects.

(2) This incendiary can be directly ignited by all igniters listed in chapter 3, coupled with a specific delay mechanism found in chapter 5. To ignite this incendiary with White Phosphorus Solution (0209), the solution must first

be poured on absorbent paper and the paper placed on top of the brick.

b. Material and Equipment.

	Parts by volume
Potassium chlorate (powdered)	40
Sulfur (powdered)	15
Granulated sugar	20
Iron filings	10
Wax (beeswax or ordinary candle wax)	15

Spoon or stick
Brick mold
Red paint
Measuring cup or can
Double boiler
Heat source (hot plate or stove)

c. Preparation.

(1) Fill the bottom half of the double boiler with water and bring to a boil.

(2) Place the upper half of the boiler on the lower portion and add the wax, sulfur, granulated sugar, and iron filings in the proper amounts.

(3) Stir well to blend all the materials evenly.

(4) Remove the upper half of the double boiler from the lower portion and either shut off the heat source or move the upper section several feet from the fire.

Caution: **Extreme care should be exercised at this point because accidental ignition of the mixture is possible. Some means of extinguishing a fire should be at hand, a fire extinguisher or sand. It is important to keep face, hands, and clothing at a reasonably safe distance during the remainder of the preparation. A face shield and fireproof gloves are recommended.**

(5) CAREFULLY add the required amount of potassium chlorate and again stir well to obtain a homogeneous mixture.

(6) Pour the mixture into a brick mold and set aside until it cools and hardens.

(7) When hard, remove the incendiary from the mold, and paint it red to simulate a normal building brick.

d. *Application.*

(1) When painted, the incendiary brick can be carried with normal construction materials and placed in or on combustible materials.

(2) A short time delay in ignition can be obtained by combining Fuse Cord (0101) or Improvised String Fuse (0102) and one of the igniter mixtures found in chapter 3. (For example, several spoonfuls of Sugar-Chlorate mixture (0201) are placed on the incendiary brick. Fuse cord is buried in the center of the igniter mixture and the fuse is taped to the brick. Delay times are determined by the length of the fuse. Suitable delay mechanisms are given in chapter 5 for delay times longer than those practical with fuse cord.)

CHAPTER 5
DELAY MECHANISMS

0401. CIGARETTE

a. Description.

(1) This item consists of a bundle of matches wrapped around a lighted cigarette. It is placed directly on easily ignited material. Ignition occurs when the lighted portion of the burning cigarette reaches the match heads. This delay mechanism can be used to initiate all igniters listed in chapter 3 except Magnesium Powder—Barium Peroxide (0210) and Powdered Aluminum—Sulfur Pellets (0207). A cigarette delay directly ignites the following incendiaries: Napalm (0301), Gelled Gasoline (exotic thickeners) (0302), and Gelled Gasoline (improvised thickeners) (0303).

(2) The following *dry* tinder type materials may also be directly ignited by the cigarette delay mechanism: Straw, paper, hay, woodshavings and rags.

(3) Usually this delay will ignite in 15 to 20 minutes, depending on length of cigarette, make of cigarette, and force of air currents. A duplicate delay mechanism should be tested to determine delay time for various ambient conditions.

(4) The cigarette must be placed so that the flame will travel horizontally or upward. A burning cigarette that is clamped or held will not burn past the point of confinement. Therefore, the cigarette should not contact any object other than matches.

b. *Material and Equipment.*
Cigarette.
Matches (wooden).
Match box.
String or tape.

c. *Preparation.*
(1) *Picket-fence delay.*

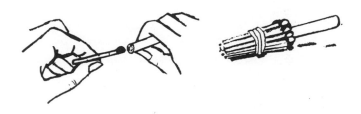

(a) Push one wooden match head into a cigarette a predetermined distance to obtain the approximate delay time.

(b) Tie or tape matches around the cigarette with the match heads at the same location as the first match in the cigarette.

(2) *Match box delay.*

Tear out one end of the inner tray of ɛ ɔox of matches (the end next to the match heads). Push one match into the cigarette. Insert this cigarette into the bunch of matches and parallel to the matches at the center of the pack. Slide the tray out of the inner box, leaving the match heads and the cigarette exposed. The head of the match in the cigarette should be even with the exposed match heads.

d. *Application.*

(1) *Picket-fence delay.*

(*a*) Light the cigarette and place the delay mechanism on a pile of igniter mixture, paper, straw, or other dry tinder type material. Be sure that the portion of the cigarette between the lit end and the match heads is not touching anything.

(*b*) Pile tinder material all around the cigarette to enhance ignition when the match heads ignite.

(2) *Match box delay.*

(*a*) Place the delay so that the cigarette is horizontal and on top of the material to be ignited. Light the cigarette.

(*b*) Be sure ignitable material such as paper, straw, flammable solvents, or napalm is placed close to the match heads. When using flammable solvents, light the cigarette away from the area of solvent fumes.

(*c*) To assure ignition of the target, sprinkle some igniter material on the combustible material. The match box delay is then placed on top of the igniter material.

0402. GELATIN CAPSULE

a. Description.

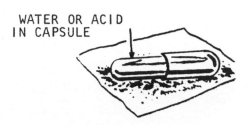

WATER OR ACID
IN CAPSULE

Gelatin capsule delays work by the action of either water or concentrated sulfuric acid on the gelatin. When the liquid dissolves the gelatin, it contacts and reacts with an igniter mix. These delays can be used with various igniters, are easily prepared and easily carried. The disadvantage is that the delay times vary with temperature and they will not work at or below 32° F. Gelatin capsule delays will work with the following igniters:

(1) Water actuated igniters such as Sugar—Sodium Peroxide (0203), Silver Nitrate—Magnesium Powder (0208), and Aluminum Powder—Sodium Peroxide (0204).

(2) Concentrated sulfuric acid actuated igniters such as Sugar-Chlorate (0201), Fire Fudge (0202), Sugar—Sodium Peroxide (0203) Aluminum Powder—Sodium Peroxide (0204), Match Head (0205), and Silver Nitrate—Magnesium Powder (0208).

b. Material and Equipment.
Concentrated sulfuric acid or water.
Gelatin capsules (1 fluid ounce capacity).

Igniter mixture.
Glass jar or bottle with glass or plastic stopper for carrying acid.

c. *Preparation.*

(1) Fill the gelatin capsule with either water or sulfuric acid, depending on which igniter is being used. Use a medicine dropper to fill the capsule. Wipe the outside of the capsule carefully and place it on a quantity of igniter mixture.

(2) Gelatin will slowly dissolve in either water or concentrated sulfuric acid, usually faster in water than in acid. Sulfuric acid should be handled carefully and only in glass or unchipped enamel containers.

d. *Application.*

(1) Fill a gelatin capsule with one of the igniter mixes listed under *Description* above. Once the liquid is added to the capsule, the next operations should be done quickly. Pile the igniter mixture on and around the capsule. Then place incendiary material in contact with the igniter mixture. (In damp weather this method should not be used with water activated igniters because premature ignition may be caused by humidity in the air.)

(2) Use the following method in damp weather. Fill a gelatin capsule with one of the igniter mixes listed above. Be sure that both halves of the capsule fit tightly and that no igniter mix is clinging to the outside of the capsule. Place the capsule in a shallow glass or porcelain dish filled with water or concentrated sulfuric acid, depending on which type of

igniter mix is used. Make sure the capsule is touching one edge of the bowl and quickly pile incendiary material close to the capsule so that when the capsule ignites, the incendiary will also ignite.

(3) The gelatin capsule delays work slowly in cold weather and will not work at or below 32° F. Capsule thickness also affects delay time. In water at 77° F.. a delay time of approximately 20 minutes can be expected, while the same type of capsule in concentrated sulfuric acid at 77° F. will give a delay time of approximately one hour. At a temperature of 50° F., the same type of capsule will give a 6 to 8 hour delay time in water and about 24 hours delay time in concentrated sulfuric acid. Delay times become less accurate at lower temperatures.

(4) The above listed delay times are given for one type of gelatin capsule only. Various types of capsules will give various delay times. Therefore, always check delay times for the capsule to be used.

(5) The sulfuric acid must be concentrated. If only battery-grade sulfuric acid is available, it must be concentrated before use to a specific gravity of 1.835 by heating it in an enameled, heat resistant glass or porcelain pot until dense, white fumes appear. See paragraph 0103 for details.

GO 7189-C

0403. RUBBER DIAPHRAGM

a. Description.

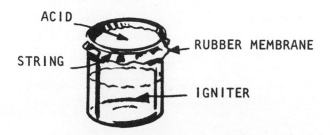

ACID

STRING

RUBBER MEMBRANE

IGNITER

(1) This delay operates by the action of concentrated sulfuric acid on a thin rubber diaphragm. As the acid eats through the diaphragm, it drips onto the igniter mix and combustion results. This delay can be used to initiate the following igniters listed in chapter 3: Sugar-Chlorate (0201), Fire Fudge (0202), Sugar—Sodium Peroxide (0203), Aluminum Powder—Sodium Peroxide (0204), Match Head (0205), Silver Nitrate—Magnesium Powder (0208), and Fire Bottle (0306).

(2) The delay does not burn or glow, a very desirable feature where premature detection may occur. The main disadvantages of this type of delay are—

(a) Delay time fluctuates with temperature changes.

(b) Delay is not reliable below 40° F.

(c) Sulfuric acid involves hazards to the operator.

b. Material and Equipment.

Concentrated sulfuric acid.

Thin rubber (such as balloons or condoms).

String, tape, or rubber bands.

Glass jar with glass stopper for carrying acid.

Wide-mouthed jar or can (approximately 1 pint capacity).

c. Preparation.

(1) Fill the wide mouth container three-quarter full with any one of the following igniter materials:

Sugar-Chlorate (0201).

Fire Fudge (0202).

Sugar—Sodium Peroxide (0203).

Aluminum Powder—Sodium Peroxide (0204).

Match Head (0205).

Silver Nitrate—Magnesium Powder (0208).

(2) Place the rubber diaphragm over the open end of the container and leave it loose enough to sag slightly into the jar. Either tie in place or secure with a rubber band.

(3) Pour about 1 fluid ounce of concentrated sulfuric acid into a small glass jar with a glass stopper and seal tightly.

d. Application.

(1) Place the jar with the rubber membrane at the desired target. Pile the material to be ignited around this jar so that when the flames issue from the jar, they will ignite the incendiary materials. *Do not put any of this igniter material on the rubber membrane.* Pour the 1 fluid ounce of concentrated sulfuric acid onto the rubber membrane. When the acid penetrates the rubber and drips onto the

102

igniter mix, a chemical reaction occurs and combustion results.

(2) The time delay of this device depends on the kind and thickness of rubber used, and on the ambient temperature. Test a similar device before actual use on the target.

(3) Using a thin rubber membrane such as a condom at a temperature of 77° F., a delay time of 15 to 20 minutes is normal. This same delay when tested at 40° F. may take as long as eight hours to penetrate the rubber membrane. Do not use this delay at temperatures below 40° F.

(4) Another simple method of using this type of delay is to first fill a small jar half full of concentrated sulfuric acid. Tie or tape a rubber membrane over the open end of the jar. BE SURE NO ACID CAN LEAK OUT. Place the bottle on its side, on top of a small pile of igniter material which will ignite on contact with the acid. When the acid penetrates the membrane, combustion will occur as before. If thicker rubber is used, stretch the rubber tightly over the mouth of the jar. This will decrease the delay time because the acid will attack the stretched rubber more effectively.

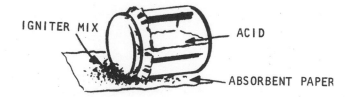

IGNITER MIX   ACID

ABSORBENT PAPER

(5) A rubber glove may also be used as a membrane for this delay. Pour some concentrated sulfuric acid into the glove and suspend the glove over a pile of igniter material. When the acid eats through the glove, it will drip onto the igniter and start a fire. A rubber glove will give a longer delay time than a condom because the material is thicker.

IGNITER MIX

(6) The rubber membranes for use in this delay must be without pin holes or other imperfections. The sulfuric acid must be *concentrated*. If only battery-grade sulfuric acid is available, it must be concentrated before use to a specific gravity of 1.835 by heating it in an enameled, heat-resistant glass or porcelain pot until dense, white fumes appear. See paragraph 0103 for details.

104

0404. PAPER DIAPHRAGM (SULFURIC ACID)

   a. Description.

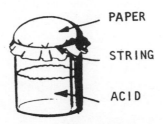

PAPER

STRING

ACID

This device consists of a half-full jar of concentrated sulfuric acid, and a paper diaphragm. The paper diaphragm is a piece of paper tied securely over the mouth of the jar. When the jar is placed on its side, the acid soaks through or corrodes the paper. The acid then contacts the igniter material and causes it to burts into flames. This delay can be used for initiating the following igniters listed in chapter 3: Sugar-Chlorate (0201), Fire Fudge (0202), Sugar—Sodium Peroxide (0203), Aluminum Powder—Sodium Peroxide (0204), Match Head (0205), Silver Nitrate—Magnesium Powder (0208).

   b. Material and Equipment
   Wide-mouthed jar.
   Sulfuric acid (concentrated).
   Paper.
   String.

   c. Preparation. Remove the cap from a wide-mouthed jar   Fill about half-full with concentrated sulfuric acid.   Tie the paper securely over the mouth of the jar.

d. Application.

(1) Make a pile of dry flammable material such as rags, papers, empty boxes, or cartons. Spread out a piece of absorbent paper on this material. Spread igniter material on the absorbent paper and place the jar (on its side) on top of the igniter material. Make certain the jar does not leak. When the acid soaks through or corrodes the paper, it will contact the igniter material and cause it to burst into flame.

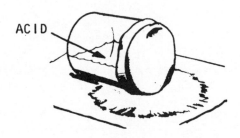

(2) This device is not reliable at temperatures below 40° F. The time delay depends on the thickness of the paper. A similar device should be tested to determine the delay provided by various thicknesses of paper. It should be tested at the temperature at which it will be used, to be sure of positive ignition. Ignition should occur in about 2 minutes at 68° F. when using writing paper. Higher ambient temperatures shorten delay times, and lower temperatures lengthen delay times.

106

0405. PAPER DIAPHRAGM (GLYCERIN)

a. *Description.*

(1) This device consists of potassium permanganate crystals wrapped in layers of absorbent paper. Glycerin is brought into contact with the wrapped potassium permanganate crystals by slowly soaking through the paper. This wets the wrapped crystals causing combustion. This delay can be used for directly initiating all igniters listed in chapter 3 except White Phosphorus (0209). The igniting ability of this delay is increased when magnesium or aluminum particles are mixed with the potassium permanganate crystals.

(2) The following incendiaries (ch 4) can be directly ignited using this delay: Napalm (0301), Gelled Gasoline (exotic thickeners) (0302), Gelled Gasoline (Improvised thickeners) (0303), Paraffin-Sawdust (0304), and Incendiary Brick (0309). Other combustible dry materials such as paper, rags, straw, and excelsior can also be directly initiated. This delay is not recommended for use in temperatures below 50° F.

b. *Material and Equipment.*

Absorbent paper (toilet paper, paper, toweling, newspaper).

Glycerin (commercial grade).

Magnesium or aluminum particles (consistency of granulated sugar).

Rubber bands or string.

Small shallow dish.

Potassium permanganate (consistency of coarse ground coffee).

Small bottle (approximately 1½ fluid ounces).

Spoon (perferably nonmetallic).

c. *Preparation.*

(1) Fill the small bottle with glycerin.

(2) Wrap a quantity of potassium permanganate crystals (a mixture of 85 parts potassium permanganate and 15 parts magnesium or aluminum particles can be substituted to produce a hotter flame) in absorbent paper. Make certain that none of the crystals fall out.

(3) The bottle and package may be carried by the person without hazard to himself, and will be available for use when needed.

d. *Application.*

(1) To use this delay, pour the glycerin into a small shallow dish or pan. Pile incendiary material around the dish so that when the glycerin ignites it will ignite the incendiary material. Place the paper container of potassium permanganate crystals into the pan of glycerin. When the glycerin soaks through the paper and contacts the potassium permanganate, ignition occurs within a few seconds.

GLYCERIN  BAG OF CRYSTALS

(2) By using various kinds of paper, different delay times can be obtained. Using more layers of paper for wrapping will increase the delay time. Using this delay at higher temperatures will also decrease the delay time. Delay times from one minute to approximately one hour are possible, depending on the conditions.

(3) The delay time should be checked under conditions which are similar to those expected at the target.

0406. CANDLE

a. *Description.*

This delay ignites flammable fuels of low volatility such as fuel oil and kerosene. A lighted candle properly inserted in a small container of flammable liquid of low volatility causes ignition of the flammable liquid when the flame burns down to the liquid level. The flame from the burning liquid is used to ignite incendiary material such as paper, straw, rags, and wooden structures. The delay time is reasonably accurate, and may be easily calibrated by determining the burning rate of the candle. No special skills are required to use this delay. Shielding is required for the candle when used in an area of strong winds or drafts. This delay is *not* recommended for use with *highly volatile liquids* because premature ignition may take place. This device is useful where a delay of one hour or longer is desired. The candle delay works well in cold or hot weather, and has the advantage of being consumed in the resulting fire, thus reducing evidence of arson.

  b. Material and Equipment.
  Candle.
  Bowl.
  Perforated can or carton.
  Fuel oil or kerosene.
  Matches.
  Small piece of cloth.

c. Preparation.
  (1) Make two marks on the side of the candle, 1½ inches and 2 inches from the top. Light the candle and record the times at which the wax melts at the marks on the side.

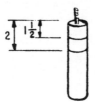

  (2) The distance burned by the candle divided by the elapsed time determines the burning rate of the candle.

d. Application.

(1) Using a lighted candle of desired length, drip hot wax in the center of the bowl. Melt the base of the candle with a lighted match. Firmly press the softened base of the candle into the hot wax in the center of the bowl. Be sure the candle will stand up sécurely without toppling over. Extinguish the candle. Wrap a small piece of cloth around the candle and slide it down to the bottom of the bowl. Place a quantity of fuel oil or kerosene in the bowl. Be sure that the level of the fluid reaches the cloth, so it will act as a wick. Pile the incendiary material around the bowl where it can catch fire after the fuel oil or kerosene ignites.

(2) If this delay must be set in a windy or drafty location, place a shield over it. Notch or punch holes in a metal can or cardboard carton at the bottom and sides for ventilation, and place this cover over the delay.

0407. OVERFLOW

a. Description.

WATER
WATER

STICK

SMALL HOLE

IGNITER MIX

This item provides a time delay in starting a fire. It consists of two tin cans, with tops removed, and uses either water or glycerin to activate the igniter material. A hole is punched in the closed end of one can. This can is placed on top of the other can which is partially filled with the liquid. The top can is completely filled with the liquid. When the bottom can fills and overflows, the overflowed liquid will react with the igniter material placed around the bottom can. This device is used for igniting the following water actuated igniters listed in chapter 3: Sugar—Sodium Peroxide (0203), Aluminum Powder—Sodium Peroxide (0204), and Silver Nitrate—Magnesium Powder (0208). Glycerin is used as the initiating liquid to ignite Potassium Permanganate glycerin (0206).

    b. Material and Equipment.

        Two tin cans.

        Nail or punch.

        Hammer.

        Water or glycerin.

        Can opener.

    c. Preparation.

    (1) Remove the tops from two cans.

    (2) Punch or drill a small hole in the closed end of one of the cans.

    (3) Partially fill the other can with either water or glycerin.

    (4) Place the can with the hole in the bottom on top of the can partially filled with igniting fluid. Insert a twig or small stick between the two cans to allow the liquid to overflow from the bottom can.

    (5) Fill the upper can with the same igniting fluid as that previously placed in the bottom can

and determine the time required for the fluid to overflow from the bottom can. If two cans of the same size are used, either one may be used for the top. If different size cans are used, place the larger can on top. The delay is variable and adjustable depending on the sizes of the cans, the quantity of liquid used, or the diameter of the hole in the top can.

d. *Application.*

(1) Always test the glycerin delay at the temperature at which it will be used. Glycerin flows slowly when cold. Do not use water in this delay near or below its freezing point, 32° F.

(2) Place the delay in the target area and fill both upper and lower cans to the desired level with the appropriate liquid.

(3) Pile igniter material around the bottom of the overflow can so the activating liquid can easily make contact with the igniter material as it flows down the side of the can.

0408. TIPPING DELAY—FILLED TUBE

a. *Description.*

VIAL OF ACID

RICE, PEAS, OR BEANS

IGNITER MIX

(1) This delay is composed of a hollow metal rod or bamboo filled with wet beans, rice or peas. The tube is inverted and placed in the center of a ring of igniter material and a small vial of water or acid is tied to the tube. When the wet beans expand, they lift and topple the tube, thereby spilling the acid or water onto the igniter causing combustion.

(2) This tipping delay may be used with a variety of igniters. They are easily prepared, and give fairly accurate delay times. This delay should not be used at temperatures near or below 32° F. when water is used as the initiator due to freezing. The following water actuated igniters listed in chapter 3 can be used with this mechanism: Sugar—Sodium Peroxide (0203), Aluminum Powder—Sodium Peroxide (0204) and Silver Nitrate—Magnesium Powder (0208). The delay may be used with concentrated sulfuric acid to initiate the above igniters .and the following acid activated igniters: Sugar-Chlorate (0201), Fire Fudge (0202), and Match Head (0205). This delay may be used with the Glycerin—Potassium Permanganate Igniter (0206).

b. *Material and Equipment.*

Metal tube, pipe or piece of bamboo closed at one end, 4 to 6 inches long and 1 inch inside diameter, or glass test tube of similar dimensions.

Small glass vial or bottle with open mouth of 1 fluid ounce capacity.

String or rubber bands.

Rice, peas, or beans.

114

Water.

Concentrated sulfuric acid.

c. Preparation. The pipe or tube may be made of any material. It must be closed at one end and flat at the other in order to stand vertically. A large glass test tube is ideal for this purpose.

    (1) Using some string or rubber bands, attach the small vial to the larger tube. Attach the vial near the top with the open end of the vial pointing up and the open end of the tube down.

TAPE

    (2) This assembly should stand up without toppling over. If it appears unsteady, move the vial downward slightly. A final adjustment may be required when the delay is filled with the required materials.

d. Application.

    (1) Rice will usually give delays of about ten to twenty minutes. Peas and beans will usually give delay times up to 4 or 5 hours. Whichever is used it must be first tested to determine the delay time for the tube that will be used.

    (2) To use this device, tightly pack the piece of pipe or bamboo with rice, peas or beans

depending on what delay time is required. Add enough water to completely moisten the beans and quickly pour off the excess water. Place the pipe open end down, and immediately fill the small vial with water or concentrated sulfuric acid, depending on which igniter is being used.

(3) Place a quantity of the igniter mixture in a ring around the delay assembly. Make the ring of such diameter that when the tube falls over, the acid or water from the vial will spill onto the igniter mixture.

(4) Place incendiary material where the flame from the igniter will start it burning.

(5) Another way in which the tipping delay can be used is to fill the small vial with glycerin instead of water or acid and then spread potassium permanganate crystals in a ring around the delay. When the glycerin is spilled onto the crystals, combustion will occur and ignite the incendiary material. The glycerin igniter will not work in temperatures below 50° F.

(6) It is recommended that this device be tested at the same temperature at which it is to be used.

0409. TIPPING DELAY—CORROSIVE OR DISSOLVING ACTION

a. Description.

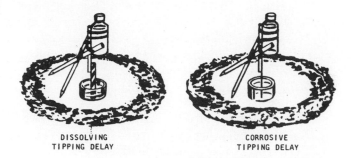

DISSOLVING
TIPPING DELAY

CORROSIVE
TIPPING DELAY

(1) This device consists of a vial of initiating liquid supported by a tripod. One of the legs which supports the vial of liquid is dissolved by a fluid. The center of gravity of the structure changes and the structure topples over. The contents of the vial spill into an appropriate igniter mixture and combustion occurs.

(2) This corrosive or dissolving tipping delay may be used with a variety of igniters. However, it should not be used at temperatures near or below 32° F. when water is used as the initiator due to freezing of the water.

(3) The following water actuated igniters listed in chapter 3 can be used with this mechanism:

Sugar—Sodium Peroxide (0203), Aluminum Powder—Sodium Peroxide (0204) and Silver Nitrate—Magnesium Powder (0208). The delay may be used with concentrated sulfuric acid to initiate the above igniters and the following acid activated igniters: Sugar-Chlorate (0201), Fire Fudge (0202), and Match Head (0205). This delay may be used with the Glycerin—Potassium Permanganate Igniter (0206)'

b. *Material and Equipment.*

Three wooden sticks or wooden pencils (approximately 6 inches long by $\frac{1}{4}$ inch diameter).

Glass vial (1 fluid ounce capacity).

String, tape or rubber bands.

Any one of the igniter mixtures mentioned above.

One of the following combination of items:

(1) Long sticks of hard candy and water.

(2) Lengths of bare copper wire and concentrated nitric acid.

(3) Iron nails or wire approximately $\frac{1}{32}$ inch diameter by 4 inches long and concentrated hydrochloric acid.

(4) Iron nails or wire and saturated cupric chloride solution.

2 glass containers with glass stoppers for carrying acid.

Shallow glass or porcelain bowl such as soup bowl or ink bottle.

c. *Preparation.*

(1) Make a tripod out of three sticks, taping them together at the top. Two legs should be the same length; the third should be about 2—3 inches shorter.

(2) Tape to the short leg, either a stick of hard candy, piece of heavy bare copper wire, steel nail, or steel wire, adjusting the length so that the wire leg stands almost vertically.

(3) The finished tripod should have a distance of about 4—5 inches between any two legs.

(4) To the top of the tripod, on the short leg, firmly tape or tie the small 1-fluide ounce capacity vial, open end up. Make certain that the tripod still stands upright after attaching the vial. The distance between legs may have to be varied to keep the tripod barely standing upright.

d. Application.

    (1) To use the delay device, insert the leg of the tripod which has the candy, wire, or nails into a glass or porcelain bowl. Fill the vial at the top of the tripod with either water, concentrated sulfuric acid, or glycerin, depending on which igniter is being used. Spread a quantity of the proper igniter material in a ring around the tripod, placing it where the spilled initiating liquid is certain to contact it. Fill the glass or porcelain bowl with the prescribed liquid for dissolving the leg of the tripod in the bowl. For hard candy the liquid is water; for copper wire the liquid is concentrated nitric acid; for steel nails the liquid may be either concentrated hydrochloric acid, or a saturated solution of cupric chloride.

    (2) No definite delay times can be established for these delays because of factors such as temperature, solution concentration, and imperfections in the leg of the tripod. Prior to use, test the device under conditions expected

at the target. The following table should be used merely as a guideline of expected delay times for the various materials.

Delay material	Delay time
Hard candy plus water_____	5—10 minutes
Copper wire plus concentrated nitric acid___	2—5 minutes
Copper wire plus nitric acid diluted with an equal volume of water.	45—60 minutes
Steel wire or nails plus concentrated hydrochloric acid.	24 hours to 7 days
Steel wire or nails plus cupric chloride solution.	10 minutes to 5—6 hours.

(3) The delay time will vary greatly with only moderate changes in temperature. Do not use this type of delay mechanism where accurate delay times are required.

0410. BALANCING STICK

a. Description.

(1) This delay device consists of a piece of wood or stick, a small vial, a nail, a piece of string, and a long strip of cloth. A hole is drilled through the middle of the stick. The vial is

fastened to one end, and the strip of cloth to the other. The length of the cloth is adjusted so that the rod just balances on a nail passing through the hole when the vial is ¾ full. The cloth is wetted with solvent to make it heavy and the vial is filled with initiating liquid to maintain balance. As the solvent evaporates, the end of the stick which supports the vial of initiating liquid becomes heavier than the end supporting the cloth. The unbalanced stick rotates about the nail until the initiating liquid spills onto the igniter mixture and combustion occurs. Fire then spreads to and ignites incendiary material.

(2) This device may be used with a variety of igniters. However, it should not be used at temperatures near or below 32° F. when water is used as the initiator due to freezing of the water. The following water actuated igniters listed in chapter 3 can be used with this mechanism: Sugar—Sodium Peroxide (0203), Aluminum Powder—Sodium Peroxide (0204) and Silver Nitrate—Magnesium Powder (0208). The device may be used with concentrated sulfuric acid to initiate the above igniters and the following acid activated igniters: Sugar-Chlorate (0201), Fire Fudge (0202), and Match Head (0205). It may also be used with the Glycerin—Potassium Permanganate Igniter (0206).

b. *Material and Equipment.*
Piece of wood (⅞ by ⅞ by 16 inches).
2 Nails.

String.

Strip of cloth.

2 glass vials (1 fluid ounce) with stoppers.

c. Preparation.

    (1) Drill a hole through the middle of the stick as shown below.

    (2) Insert a nail through the hole. The nail should permit the stick to turn freely. Tie a piece of string (4–6 inches in length) to both ends of the nail, forming a loop. It is not important that the stick balance exactly.

    (3) To one end of the stick tape a small glass vial. Tilt the vial when attaching it so that when this end of the stick is about 8 inches above the other end, the vial will be vertically upright. On the other end of the stick tie a strip of cloth, rag, or rope. This strip should be heavy enough so that the stick is balanced when the vial is about ¾ full of initiating fluid.

VIAL

STRING

d. Application.

(1) To use this delay, drive a nail (approximately 4 inches long) into a wall or wooden box about 8 inches above the floor, leaving at least 2 inches of the nail projecting. Place the loop of string on the nail near the head of the nail. The stick should not touch the box or wall, but must swing freely. The rag should touch the floor. Pour enough solvent on the rag to soak it thoroughly (approximately 1 fluid ounce). Working quickly, fill the vial with initiating liquid and balance the rod by shifting the cloth. Spread a quantity of appropriate igniter mixture on the floor where the initiating liquid will spill when the solvent on the cloth evaporates. In a few minutes the solvent will evaporate, causing the stick to become unbalanced. The vial will tilt with the stick and, the liquid in the vial will pour out and initiate the igniter mixture.

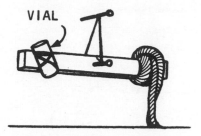

VIAL

(2) Where no solvent is available or where the odor of solvent may make the device easy to detect, do not use cloth soaked with solvent. Use a wire basket containing ice as shown below.

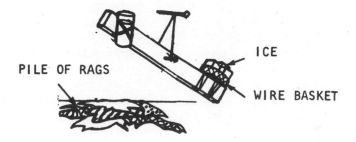

ICE

PILE OF RAGS

WIRE BASKET

(3) When ice is used, the delay time will be a matter of minutes, depending on the ambient temperature. Ice cannot be used at temperatures near 32° F. Be sure that the drippings from the melting ice does not wet the igniter or interfere with initial combustion of flammable material.

0411. STRETCHED RUBBER BAND

a. Description.

RUBBER BAND

IGNITER MIX

ACID

STICK

This item utilizes a rubber band, which has been soaked in gasoline or carbon disulfide until it has considerably expanded. After removal of the rubber band from the solvent, the rubber band is attached to a wall and to a bottle containing igniter fluid. As the rubber band contracts due to solvent evaporation, the bottle is tipped and initiator liquid comes in contact with an appropriate igniter material. This stretched rubber band delay may be used with a variety of igniters. However, it should not be used at temperatures near or below 32° F. when water is used as the initiator because the water freezes. The following water actuated igniters listed in chapter 3 can be used with this mechanism: Sugar—Sodium Peroxide (0203), Aluminum Powder—Sodium Peroxide (0204), and Silver Nitrate—Magnesium Powder (0208). The delay may be used with concentrated sulfuric acid to initiate the above igniters and the following acid activated igniters: Sugar-Chlorate (0201), Fire Fudge (0202), and Match Head (0205). This delay may be used with Glycerin—Potassium Permanganate Igniter (0206).

b. Material and Equipment.
Bottle or jar (1 to 2 fluid ounce capacity).
Rubber bands.
Gasoline or carbon disulfide.
Air tight container for carrying the gasoline or carbon disulfide.
Nails.
Igniter.

c. Preparation.
(1) Fill a bottle (1 to 2 fluid ounce capacity) with water, acid, or glycerin, depending on which igniter is to be used.
(2) Soak the rubber bands in gasoline or carbon disulfide for about one hour. Do not soak too long or they will become excessively weakened.

d. Application.
(1) At the place where the delay is to be used, drive a large headed nail into the wall, leaving about 2 to 2½ inches exposed. Loop the rubber bands over the head of the nail. Place the bottle two bottle heights away from the nail. Quickly loop the free end of the rubber bands over the neck of the bottle. Move the bottle back and forth until there is just enough tension in the rubber bands to hold the bottle without it toppling when a pencil or twig is placed under the far end. The stick under the end of the bottle is used as a tilt device to make sure that the bottle topples over when the rubber band contracts.
(2) Place some incendiary material close to the bottle. Sprinkle a quantity of igniter mixture about the area in which the liquid will be spilled. As the solvent evaporates, the rubber

bands will shrink, tip the bottle, spill the
liquid, and initiate the igniter material.
Note. Always set up the bottle before spreading the
igniter mixture.

0412. ALARM CLOCK

a. Description.

(1) This device is used for igniting materials after
a definite delay time. The device employs a
manually-wound alarm clock, with the alarm
bell removed, as the timing mechanism. A
piece of string is fastened to the key used to
wind the alarm. The other end of the string is
fastened to a bottle of appropriate initiating
liquid. When the modified alarm mechanism
is tripped, the winding key will reel in the
string and overturn the bottle of initiating
liquid and start a fire.

(2) This alarm clock delay may be used with a
variety of igniters. However, it should not
be used at temperatures near or below 32° F.
when water is used as the initiator because the
water freezes. The following water actuated

igniters listed in chapter 3 can be used with this mechanism: Sugar—Sodium Peroxide (0203), Aluminum Powder—Sodium Peroxide (0204), and Silver Nitrate—Magnesium Powder (0208). The delay may be used with concentrated sulfuric acid to initiate the above igniters and the following acid activated igniters: Sugar-Chlorate (0201), Fire Fudge (0202), and Match Head (0205). This delay may be used with Glycerin—Potassium Permanganate (0206).

(3) This device will produce fairly accurate delay times between one and eleven hours.

Caution: **The ticking sound of the clock may reveal the presence of the device.**

b. *Material and Equipment.*
Alarm clock, manually wound (without bell, if possible).
Bottle.
String.
Initiator liquid.
Cloth or absorbent paper.

c. *Preparation.*
(1) Remove the bell or striker from the clock.
(2) Fully wind time and alarm springs.
(3) Set desired time on alarm.
(4) Tie the string to the alarm key so that it will be pulled when the alarm mechanism is tripped. If necessary, tie a twig or stick to the alarm key to obtain a longer level.

d. *Application.*
(1) Tie the string to the alarm key or stick. Set the clock in place and anchor it if necessary. Muffle the clock with rags, making sure that

the rags do not interfere with the reeling action of the alarm mechanism. Tie the free end of the string to the bottle of activating liquid. The bottle should be tilted in the direction of the fall by a pencil or twig. When this device is placed on a smooth surface, the clock should be taped, tied, or weighted down to prevent it from sliding when the tension in the string is taken up by the revolving key.

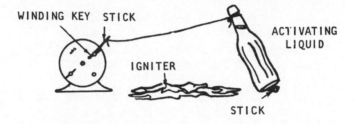

WINDING KEY STICK

ACTIVATING LIQUID

IGNITER

STICK

(2) Adjust the spacing so that the string is taut. Place a cloth or an absorbent paper towel where the contents of the bottle will be spilled. Place a quantity of igniter mixture on the cloth or paper towel. Partially overlap the igniter mixture with a flammable material so as to assist combustion.

CHAPTER 6
SPONTANEOUS COMBUSTION

0501. SPONTANEOUS COMBUSTION

a. Description.

(1) Spontaneous combustion is the outbreak of fire in combustible material that occurs without application of direct flame or spark. A combustible material such as cotton waste, sawdust, or cotton batting is impregnated with a mixture of a vegetable oil and specific drying oils known as driers. This impregnated combustible material is placed in a container which provides confinement around the sides and bottom. Heat produced by the chemical action of the driers in the oil is transferred to the confined combustible material with resultant outbreak of fire. Prepared igniter materials such as Fire Fudge (0202) or initiator material such as Fuse Cord (0101) can be used with the impregnated combustible material to increase reliability and decrease ignition delay time.

(2) The chemical reaction that supplies heat in the spontaneous combustion device becomes faster as the surrounding temperature rises. Conversely, as the temperature drops ignition delay time increases. In addition, ignition delay time varies somewhat with type of

vegetable oil, type of drier, type of combustible material, confinement, density of the oil impregnated combustible material, and ventilation. Devices planned for use should be tried in advance to establish delay time.

(3) These devices operate with a natural delay caused by the chemical reaction time of the drying process in the oil. The user places the device and is away from the scene when the fire starts. Spontaneous combustion devices have the added advantage of using items seen daily around shop, plant, or office. Containers for confining the impregnated combustible material can be small waste paper baskets, packing boxes, ice cream containers, paper bags and other items common to a particular operation. Combustible materials such as cotton waste, cotton batting, or sawdust are also common in many manufacturing plants. For these reasons, spontaneous combustion devices are useful and clever sabotage items.

(4) It is recommended that these devices be covertly used to ignite readily flammable material such as rags, dry paper, dry hay, wooden and cardboard boxes, wooden structures, and other similar targets.

b. Material and Equipment.

Ingredient	Used for	Common source
Vegetable Oils		
Boiled linseed oil___	Paint manufacture__	Hardware stores
Raw linseed oil____	Paint manufacture__	Hardware stores
Safflower oil_____	Food_____	Drug and food stores
Tung oil (China wood).	Paint manufacture__	Paint manufacturers

132

Ingredient	Used for	Common source
Driers		
Cobalt (6%)_____	Paint manufacture__	Paint manufacturers
Lead (24%)_____	Paint manufacture__	Paint manufacturers
Manganese (can be substituted for cobalt).		
Lead oxide (can be substituted for lead).		
Combustible Materials		
Cotton waste_____	Machine shops, maintenance shops.	By-product of textile manufacture.
Cotton batting____	Furniture manufacture.	Felt & textile manufacturers.
Sawdust_____	Water-oil-grease absorbent.	By-product of food working.
Kapok_____	Life jackets, furniture padding, bedding.	Furniture manufacturers, food products manufacturers.
Miscellaneous Items		
Cardboard or paper container.	General_____	Commonly available
Stick approximately 1½ inches in diameter.	General_____	Commonly available
Sharp knife_____	General_____	Commonly available
One pint wide-mouth jar.	General_____	Commonly available
Teaspoon_____	General_____	Commonly available
Fire Fudge Igniter (optional).	Igniter_____	See paragraph 0202
Fuse Cord (optional).	Initiator_____	See paragraph 0101

Proportions of Mixture

System	*Vegetable oil*	*Cobalt drier (teaspoon)*	*Lead drier (teaspoon)*	*Combustible material (tightly packed)*
1	Boiled linseed oil, 1/3 pint.	1/2	2	Cotton waste, 1 pint.
2	Boiled linseed oil, 1/3 pint.	1/2	2	Cotton batting, 3 pints.
3	Boiled linseed oil, 1/3 pint.	1/2	2	Sawdust, 1 pint
4	Boiled linseed oil, 1/3 pint.	1/2	2	Kapok, 1 pint
5	Raw linseed oil, 1/3 pint.	1	4	Kapok, 1 pint
6	Safflower oil, 1/3 pint.	1/2	2	Cotton waste, 1 pint.
7	Safflower oil, 1/3 pint.	1/2	2	Cotton batting, 3 pints.
8	Safflower oil, 1/3 pint.	1/2	2	Sawdust, 1 pint
9	Safflower oil, 1/3 pint.	1/2	2	Kapok, 1 pint
10	Tung oil, 1/3 pint	1/2	2	Cotton waste, 1 pint.
11	Tung oil, 1/3 pint	1/2	2	Cotton batting, 3 pints.
12	Tung oil, 1/3 pint	1/2	2	Sawdust, 1 pint
13	Tung oil, 1/3 pint	1/2	2	Kapok, 1 pint

Note. The above quantities for each system are approximately correct for use in a 1 gallon confinement container. The impregnated combustible material should fill the container to approximately 1/3 to 1/2 the volume for best results. Different size containers can be used with properly adjusted quantities of impregnated combustible material. At approximately 70° F., delay time to ignition is roughly 1 to 2 hours. With Fire Fudge or Fuse Cord added to the impregnated combustible material, delay time is reduced to roughly 1/2 to 1 hour. The exception to this is System 8 where delay time to ignition is about 2 to 3 hours. With Fire Fudge or Fuse Cord added, delay time is shortened to 1 to 2 hours.

c. Preparation.

(1) *General instructions.*

(*a*) Measure the combustible material by tightly packing it up to the top of the one pint measuring jar. The material should puff out of the measuring jar when firm hand pressure is removed.

(*b*) Transfer the combustible material from the measuring jar to the container in which it is to be confined.

(*c*) Pour the vegetable oil into the one pint measuring jar to one-third jar volume.

(*d*) Using a teaspoon, add the specified quantity of Cobalt Drier to the vegetable oil in the one pint measuring jar. Wipe the spoon dry and add the specified quantity of Lead Drier to the Vegetable Oil—Cobalt Drier mixture.

(*e*) Thoroughly mix the combination of vegetable oil and driers by stirring with the teaspoon for approximately one minute.

Note. Vegetable oil and drier can be mixed and stored in an air-tight container for one week before use. Longer storage is not recommended.

(*f*) Pour the oil mixture from the one pint measuring jar over the combustible material in the container. Saturate the combustible material by kneading, pulling and balling with the hands. This can be accomplished either inside or outside of the container.

(g) Remove saturated combustible material from the container.

(h) Cut a hole with a knife, one to two inches in diameter, in the bottom center of the container.

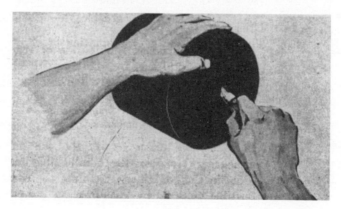

(i) Place the container on a flat surface, hold the 1½-inch diameter stick vertically over the hole in the bottom of the container and pack the saturated combustible material

around the stick compressing it so that it
fills ⅓ to ½ of the container volume after
hand pressure is removed.

(j) Remove the stick. This leaves a ventilation hole through the center of the combustible material. The spontaneous combustion device is now ready for use unless
the following optional step is taken.

(k) This step is optional. *Either* take a piece
of Fire Fudge (0202) about the size of a
walnut and crush it into pieces about the
size of peas. Sprinkle the pieces of crushed
Fire Fudge on top of the combustible

material. *Or* cut a piece of Fuse Cord (0101) to a length of about four inches. Since safety fuse burns inside the wrapping, it is sliced in half to expose the black powder. (Lacquer coated fuse (nonsafety type) burns completely and may be used without slicing.) Insert one or more pieces of fuse vertically in the combustible materiel near the center vent hole, leaving about one inch extending out of the top surface of the combustible material.

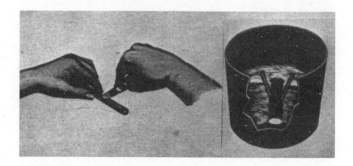

(2) *Preparation of improvised driers.* If the commercial driers (cobalt and lead) specified under *Material and Equipment* above are not available, the following improvised driers can be made using either flashlight batteries or powdered lead oxide (Pb_3O_4). These improvised driers are used in the same manner as the commercial driers.

(a) *Manganese drier.*

1. Break open three flashlight batteries (size

TAGO 7189-C

D) and collect the pasty material surrounding the central carbon rod.

2. Put this material in a one-pint wide-mouth jar and fill jar with water.

3. Slowly stir contents of jar for approximately two minutes and allow contents to settle. The contents will usually settle in one-half hour.

4. Pour off water standing on top of settled contents.

5. Remove wet contents from jar, spread it on a paper towel and allow to dry.

6. Dry the jar.

7. Pour raw linseed oil into the one-pint measuring jar to one-third jar volume.

8. Combine the measured quantity of raw linseed oil and the dried battery contents from 5 above in a pot and boil for one-half hour.

9. Shut off heat, remove pot from the heat source, and allow the mixture to cool to room temperature.

10. Separate the liquid from the solid material settled on the bottom by carefully pouring the liquid into a storage bottle. Discard the solid material. The liquid is the drier.

11. The manganese drier is ready for use.

12. If manganese dioxide powder is available, flashlight batteries need not be used. Place one heaping teaspoonful of manganese dioxide powder into the raw linseed oil and boil the mixture in a pot for one-half hour. Then follow 9, 10, and 11 above.

(b) *Lead oxide drier.*
  1. Pour raw linseed oil into the one-pint measuring jar to one-third jar volume.
  2. Combine the measured quantity of raw linseed oil and two heaping teaspoonfuls of lead oxide in a pot and boil gently for one-half hour. The mixture must be stirred constantly to avoid foaming over.
  3. Shut off heat, remove pot from the heat source, and allow the mixture to cool to room temperature.
  4. Pour the liquid into a storage bottle and cap the bottle.
  5. The lead oxide drier is ready for use.
d. *Application.*
  (1) The spontaneous combustion device is placed at the target on a flat surface with one edge propped up to allow ventilation through the impregnated combustible material.

Since flames normally shoot up from the open top of the container, combustible target material should be positioned from three to five inches directly over the top of the device for satisfactory ignition of the target. *DO NOT COVER OPEN TOP OF CONTAINER.*

(2) Temperature of the environment in which these devices are used affect, the ignition time these devices are used affects the ignition time. The following table gives approximate time to ignition at different temperatures. However, it is recommended that ignition time be determined by advance trial.

Temperature (° F.)	Time to ignition (hours)
60–70	1–2
40–60	2–4
30–40	4–10

(3) Spontaneous combustion devices can also be improvised by stuffing impregnated combustible material into a pocket of any one of the following garments: coat, laboratory jacket, pants, or similar items. The combustible material stuffed in the pocket should be below the top of the pocket and should not be packed too tight.

TAGO 7189-C

INDEX

By Order of the Secretary of the Army:

HAROLD K. JOHNSON,
General, United States Army,
Official: *Chief of Staff.*
J. C. LAMBERT,
Major General, United States Army,
The Adjutant General.

☆ U. S. GOVERNMENT PRINTING OFFICE : 1967 O - 300-528 (7016C)

IMPROVISED INCENDIARIES
General

Good incendiaries can be improvised more easily than explosives and the materials are more easily obtained. On a pound for pound basis, incendiaries can do more damage than explosives against many type targets if properly used. There is a time lag, however, between the start of a fire and the destruction of the target. During this period the fire may be discovered and controlled or put out. An explosive once detonated has done its work.

Incendiaries are cheap and little training is needed for their preparation and use. Used in very carefully excuted operations, the act of sabotage may be concealed in the ashes of an "accidental" fire.

Fires may be started quickly and have reasonable chance of success if the following few simple principles are observed:

1. See that there is plenty of air and fuel to feed the fire.

2. Use an incendiary that supplies a prolonged and persistent heat.

3. Start the fire low in the target structure and let it spread naturally upwards.

4. Use reflecting surfaces, such as corners, boxes, shelves, to concentrate the heat.

5. Use drafts to spread the fire rapidly — near stairways, elevator shafts.

6. Protect the fire from discovery during the first few minutes by good concealment and timing.

In preparing improvised incendiaries observe basic rules of safety. Chemicals that must be powered should be ground separately with clean tools and then mixed in the indicated proportions. Chemicals or mixtures should be kept tightly sealed in jars or cans to protect them from moisture. Damp materials will work poorly if at all.

Sulfuric acid, which is useful for chemical delays and to ignite incendiaries or explosive detonators, can be obtained by concentrating battery acid. This can be done by boiling off the water in the battery acid in a glass or porcelained pan until dense white fumes begin to appear. This operation should be done out of doors and the resulting concentrated acid should be handled carefully.

The paragraphs which follow will describe the preparation of several igniter (or "first fire") incendiary mixes, some basic incendiary mixes, and a thermate metal-destroying incendiary.

The subject of incendiaries has been treated much more exhaustively in other publications. The intent of this handbook is to provide only a few techniques.

147

Potassium Chlorate and Sugar Igniter

Chlorate-sugar is one of the best of the first fire or igniter mixes. It burns very rapidly, with a yellow-white flame, and generates sufficient heat to ignite all homemade incendiaries mentioned in this handbook.

MATERIALS: Potassium chlorate (preferred) or sodium chlorate, sugar.

PREPARATION:

1. Grind the chlorate separately in a clean, non-sparking (glass or wooden) bowl with a wooden pestle. the resulting granules should approximate those of ordinary table sugar.

2. Mix equal volumes of the granulated chlorate and sugar by placing both on a large sheet of paper and then lifting the corners alternately.

CAUTION: This mixture is extremely spark sensitive and must be handled accordingly.

3. Wrap 4 to 6 tablespoonfuls of the mixture in thin paper so as to form a tight packet. Keep the mixture as dry as possible. If it is to be stored in a damp area before using, the packet may be coated with paraffin wax.

Chlorate-sugar is easily ignited by the flame of a match, the spit of a percussion cap or time fuse, with concentrated sulfuric acid.

If ignited when under confinement it will explode like gunpowder. If it is contained in a waxed packet, therefore, the latter should be punched through in several places before it is used with a basic incendiary and ignited.

Flake Aluminum-Sulfur Igniter

This simple igniter burns extremely hot and will ignite even the metal-destroying thermate, described later on. The mixture itself can be lit by chlorate-sugar.

MATERIALS: Flake aluminum, finely powdered sulfur.

PREPARATION:

1. Mix 4 parts by volume of finely powdered sulfur with 1 part of aluminum powder.

To use, place several spoonfuls of the mixture on the material to be lit and add a spoonful of chlorate-sugar on top. Be sure the safety (time) fuse or other spark-producing delay system is placed so it will act upon the chlorate-sugar mixture first.

Homemade Black Powder Igniter

Black powder may be used for igniting napalm, flammable solvents in open containers, paper, loose rags, straw, excelsior and other tinder type materials. If it is not available already mixed, it can be prepared as follows:

MATERIALS: Potassium (or sodium) nitrate, powdered charcoal. powdered sulfur, powde)

PREPARATION:

1. Into a clean, dry jar or can put 7 spoonfuls of potassium or sodium nitrate, 2 spoonfuls of powdered charcoal, and 1 spoonful of powdered sulfur. The ingredients must be at least as fine as granulated sugar. If they must be ground, GRIND EACH SEPATATELY. Never grind the mixed ingredients — they may ignite or explode.

2. Cap the can or jar tightly and shake and tumble it until the ingredients are completely mixed.

The mixture will be effective for months if kept tightly sealed and dry. Sodium nitrate in particular has a tendency to absorb moisture.

To use the gunpowder, pile 2 or 3 spoonfuls on top of any solid incendiary material which is to be ignited. For igniting liquids in open containers, wrap 2 or 3 spoonfuls in a piece of paper and suspend it just above the liquid.

Gunpowder is best ignited by safety fuse. It burns very quickly and with a great deal of heat, so allow sufficient time delay for safe withdrawal from the vicinity.

Match Head Igniter

A good ignition material for incendiaries can be obtained from the heads of safety matches, which are available almost any place. The composition must be removed from the heads of many of them to get a sufficient quantity of igniter material. It will ignite napalm, wax and sawdust, paper, and other flammables.

MATERIALS: Safety matches.

PREPARATION:

Remove the match head composition by scraping with a knife or crushing with pliers. Collect several spoonfuls of it and store in a moisture-tight container.

Put at least 2 spoonfuls on the material to be ignited. To ignite liquids, such as solvents or napalm, wrap several spoonfuls in a piece of paper and hang this just over the fluid, or place nearby. If fluids dampen the mixture it may not ignite.

Ignition can be by time fuse, fircracker fuse, a spark, or concentrated sulfuric acid.

Time Fuse Fire Starter

Several igniters or first fire mixes can be set off by a spark from time fuse. Others require a stronger flame. Time fuse, plus matches, can be combined to improve this more intense initial flame.

MATERIALS: Time (safety) fuse, safety matches, string or tape.

PREPARATION:

1. About ¼ inch from the end of a piece of time fuse cut a notch with a sharp knife so that the powder train is exposed.

2. Around the fuse at this point tape or tie several matches so that their heads are in contact with each other and at least one match head is directly over the notch. See Figure 59.

When the fuse burns down, a spark from the notch ignites the one match head, which flares and ignites the others. this fire starter can be inserted into an igniter mix or used alone to light crumped paper or excelsior. Another application, nonelectric firing of the 3.5" rocket, is described earlier.

Homemade Napalm

Napalm is the best incendiary to use against most flammable targets. It will readily ignite paper, straw, flammable solvents, or wooden structures.

MATERIALS: Gasoline or fuel oil, nondetergent soap (bar, flakes, or powder).

PREPARATION:

1. Use about equal parts of soap and oil. If bar soap is used, slice it into small chips. If both gasoline and fuel oil are available, use both in equal parts.

2. Heat the fuel in an open container, preferably one with a handle, out of doors. Try to avoid creating sparks or having a high open flame, but if the fuel should catch on fire extinguish it by placing a board or piece of tin over the container.

3. Gasoline, in particular, will begin to bubble very quickly. When it does, remove from the fire and gradually add the soap, stirring continuously, until the soap is completely dissolved and a thin pasty liquid results. If necessary return the mixture to the fire, but as a safety measure it is best not to stir while the container is on the fire.

4. When the desired consistency is reached allow the mixture to cool.

5. Napalm also can be mixed by a cold method, although it may take hours to thicken. This should be done by alternately adding very small amounts of soap chips or powder and gasoline or fuel oil and stirring until the mixture reaches a thin jelly-like consistency. It is best to start with

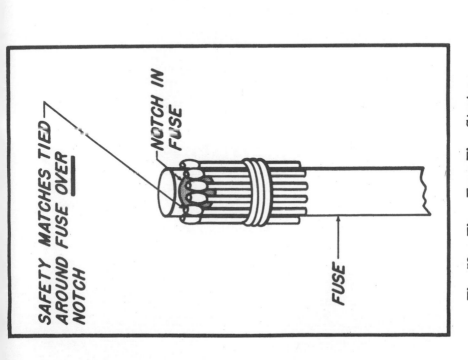

RAG STOPPER

HOMEMADE NAPALM

Fig. 60 — Molotov Cocktail

SAFETY MATCHES TIED AROUND FUSE OVER NOTCH

NOTCH IN FUSE

FUSE

Fig. 59 — Time Fuse Fire Starter

about a cupful of soap, add part of a cup of solvent and stir that until smooth before gradually adding the remaining ingredients. Continuous stirring is not required. In fact, it is advisable just to let the mixture and the mixer rest from time to time and give the soap a chance to dissolve.

Napalm will keep well if stored in a tightly sealed container. It can be ignited with a match or any of the first fire mixtures described previously. The ignition packet should be placed adjacent to or just over the napalm, otherwise the petroleum may soak it and prevent its burning.

When napalm is used on easily ignitible materials (such as loosely piled paper, rags, or hay) it should be spread out so it will start a large area burning at once. Tightly baled paper or rags should be loosened first, because they do not burn well. If used directly against wooden structures or other large articles which are diffcult to ignite, the napalm should be concentrated in sufficient quantity to provide a hot, long lasting blaze. If about a half dozen pieces of charcoal are put into and around the napalm the heat output is considerably increased.

Napalm makes an excellent "Molotov cocktail." Just fill any glass bottle with a small neck with the napalm and cram a twisted strip of cloth into the mouth of the bottle as a stopper. See Figure 60. When ready to use, pull about 4 to 6 inches of the rag stopper out of the bottle. Light the napalm-soaked rag with a match and, when the rag is burning well, throw the bottle at the target. When the bottle breaks napalm spashes over the target and is ignited by the burning rag.

Paraffin-Sawdust Incendiary

Paraffin-sawdust is almost as effective as napalm against combustible targets, but it is slower in starting. It is solid when cool and thus is more easily carried and used than liquid napalm. In addition, it can be stored indefinitely without special care.

MATERIALS: Dry sawdust, paraffin, beeswax, or candle wax.

PREPARATION:

1. Melt the wax, remove the container from the fire and stir in a roughly equal amount of sawdust.

2. Continue to stir the cooling mixture until it becomes almost solid, then remove from the container and let it cool and solidify further.

Lumps of the mixture the size of a fist are easiest to manage. The chunks of incendiary may be carried to the target in a paper bag or other wrapper. Any igniter that will set fire to the paper wrapper will ignite the wax and sawdust.

A similar incendiary can be made by dipping sheets of newspaper into melted wax and allowing them to cool. These papers may then be crumpled up and used in the same manner as the paraffin-sawdust, although they will not burn as hot and persistently.

Sawdust, Moth Flakes, and Oil Incendiary

This incendiary is very good for use against all kinds of wooden structures, including heavy beams and timbers. It also works well on paper, rags, straw, excelsior, and other tinder type materials. It will start fires in open containers of flammable liquids, piles of coal, coke, or lumber, and on baled rags and paper. It is not effective against metal.

MATERIALS: Dry sawdust, moth flakes (naphthalene), fuel oil (kerosene or diesel oil).

PREPARATION:

1. Place equal parts of sawdust, moth flakes, and oil into a container and stir until the mixture is the consistency of mush.

2. Store it in any container that will retain the oil fumes.

An easy, effective way to use this mixture is to put about a quart of it in a paper bag and place the bag on the target material. The bag can be lit with a match and the mixture will ignite quite readily. It burns as well as napalm. If a longer delay time is required, use one of the igniter mixes described earlier along with time fuse or other delay device. The time fuse alone, however, will not ignite the incendiary mix.

Where very large wood beams are to be burned, an additional amount of the incendiary will be required. Two or three quarts is enough to destroy almost any target against which the technique would be effective.

For the greatest effect on wooden structures, the mixture should be in a pile, never spread out in a thin layer. It should be placed beneath the target material, if possible, so the flames will spread upward. In a packing box or room, a corner is a good place to start the fire.

Thermate Incendiary

Thermate is similar to commercial thermit, used in welding, except that it also contains an oxidizer, making it easier to ignite. Thermate will readily burn paper, rags, excelsior, straw, and other tinder type materials. However, its main use in sabotage operations is against motors, gears, lathes, or other metal targets — to weld moving parts together, warp precision machined surfaces, and so on. Since it burns with a brief, almost explosive action, it is not recommended for burning wooden structures or other materials where persistent heat is required.

A good source of ready-made thermate is the U.S. military AN M-14 Incendiary Grenade. To remove the thermate, first pry out the fuse assembly with crimpers or other nonsparking implement. See Figure 61. The reddish-brown caked substance on top of the contents of the grenade is a first fire mixture and it is spark sensitive. This should be broken up and the grayish powder beneath, which is the thermate, can be poured out.

Thermate also can be made from aluminum or magnesium powder and a chemical oxidizing agent, as described below:

MATERIALS: Aluminum filings, powder or flakes, or magnesium filings or powder, plus any one of the following chemicals: potassium nitrate, sodium nitrate, barium nitrate, potassium dichromate, sodium dichromate, or potassium permanganate. Although aluminum and magnesium are equally effective, thermate made from magnesium is easier to ignite. Flake aluminum, which is the extremely fine variety used in paints, is excellent. In any case, both the metal and chemical ingredients should be no coarser than granulated sugar.

PREPARATION:

1. Fill a quart size (or larger) container about 2/3 full of equal parts of the metal powder and the oxidizing agent.

2. Cover with a tight lid, then roll and tumble the container until the contents are completely mixed.

3. If flake aluminum is the metal used, fill the container ½ full of the aluminum then add oxidizing agent until the container is ¾ full. Mix as described above.

Thermate in a sealed container can be stored for months. To use, put 1 or 2 pounds of the mixture in a paper bag and place it on the target in such a way that when it burns the red hot molten material will run down and attack the vital parts.

Chlorate-sugar and aluminum-sulfur igniters are best for setting off thermate, particularly if the thermate contains aluminum powder, which is more difficult to ignite.

Thermate also is used in the improvised dust initiator and the external POL charges described later.

THERMATE GRENADE

FUSE

CRIMPER

Fig. 61 — Defusing Thermate Grenade